DID THE VIRGI
AND DIE IN ENGLAND?

FROM FLOATING THE, SEEMINGLY IMPROBABLE, PROPOSITION THAT MARY THE MOTHER OF JESUS LIVED A CONSIDERABLE, PERHAPS THE MAJOR, PART OF HER LIFE IN BRITAIN AND IS BURIED HERE TO ACCEPTING THAT PROPOSITION AS A FACT IS A LONG, EXCITING AND FASCINATING JOURNEY.

DID THE VIRGIN MARY LIVE AND DIE IN ENGLAND?

by
Victor Dunstan

GROSVENOR HOUSE,
20 ST. ANDREWS CRESCENT,
CARDIFF, SOUTH WALES, G.B.

ISBN 0946922 60 8
Published by Megiddo Press Limited
in conjunction with The Dunstan Foundation.

CONTENTS

1 The First Christmas – How Much Is Fact And How Much Fiction?

About forty eight years AFTER Julias Caesar set foot on the shores of Britain an event took place in Bethlehem of Judea which was to change the face of the world for ever.

It is said, and many still believe it, that a virgin gave birth to a son — he who was to be called THE SON OF GOD! He was to minister for about a year, some think three years, and was to die the unexceptional death of thousands of criminals, the death of crucifixion.

Stripped of the element of faith, and the aura which surrounds him as a result of several million sermons and books, books enough, had one of each publication been preserved, to fill a library of considerable proportions, he was an unexceptional man who said little that was new or revolutionary.

Yet it took him only one year to transform the world and persuade not only the humble and illiterate but also the intelligensia of all generations that God did manifest Himself in the flesh in HIS person.

The year was B.C.7 (not A.D.1 as has been mistakenly believed) and the 15 year old Virgin Mary was betrothed to a carpenter, many years her senior, by the name of Joseph. It was Joseph's second marriage.

It would seem that, when the pregnancy was made known to him, Joseph was not at all happy and not a little suspicious, which is what one would expect in view of the strict moral codes which existed in the community in which he lived at the time.

Then, as now, God was blamed for a lot of things which He had not caused to happen and the pregnancy of unmarried mothers was often one of them. Because the penalties for fornication were severe, often death, few young women freely admitted that they had had an enjoyable cohabitation, preferring rather to blame the coming unhappy event on the good old stand-by rape — or God!

The story which we will see unfold in this book will be the more fascinating and the more exciting if we are able first of all to examine what we REALLY believe about the Christmas story. Denuded of any covering of faith, what is demonstrably true about it?

Unfortunately we, brought up under Christian influence, are apt to accept Christmas as being part of life's scenery and we can no more imagine Christmas without the Virgin birth than we can accept a boiled egg without toast soldiers.

We do not, most of us, worry overmuch whether the unimaginable events of that first Christmas actually took place. We would rather not delve too deeply for fear of upsetting our image of something we would PREFER to believe. As when we watch a film we would like to be true, we hold in suspension our critical faculties and question not, preferring rather to enjoy as an emotional experience, and perhaps as a parable for living, that 'mash' of Dickens, Scrooge, commercialism and the nativity which our Christmas has become. Apart from those few 'wits' among us who dare to parody the carols with 'Hark, the happy till bells ring' and the like we unthinkingly do all the things that devoted Christmas disciples are supposed to do.

But did it all REALLY happen? Was there really a Star of Bethlehem? Did God actually father a human child — do YOU really believe He did? Did supernatural voices proclaim that salvation had reached down to man? Or was Jesus the illegitimate son of a Roman soldier as many of the Jews of his time contented? In fact is anything of the Christmas story true and if so, how much of it?

THE STAR OF BETHLEHEM

When I was a child, a favourite pastime around Christmas was to look heavenwards on a frosty night and see if we could see the 'Star of Bethlehem'. Of course we often did, because part of the magic of childhood is that it is often possible to see exactly what one expects to see.

Someone once said that we all become children at Christmas, and perhaps it is inevitably so, for no story has so moved the world as the story of the babe in the manger at Bethlehem. At Christmas, reason takes a holiday and we question not whether herald angels did actually appear in the shepherd's fields at Bethlehem: The antiseptic manger and the obligatory halos seem somehow to be right, and the star of Bethlehem somehow fits snuggly into the pattern, along with Father Christmas and the plum pudding. Few, I think, give much thought as to whether a star did actually go before the wise men as they made their way towards the place where Jesus was born.

Though I do not wish to debunk Christmas, it is far too nice a festival for that, I would like to ask you, my reader, if you really DO believe the Christmas story as historic fact as distinct from believing the Christmas message, which, I hope, we all believe.

The star of Bethlehem is a very important part of the Christmas story.

The star the wise men are said to have followed to Bethlehem is, yes, and demands to be, depicted on all the Christmas paraphernalia. What would Christmas be without the star on the tree, the star on the card and the star dangling from the ceiling? What would the nativity play be without the wise men, colourful all, who follow the star? It's wonderful, magical and scintillating. But did it happen or is it just a pleasant myth? You see, the veracity of the prophets depends upon that star, for, if they have inserted one such bit of nonsense into their writings 'bang' goes their claim to divine inspiration! We all like fairy stories, but who wants a prophet who creates fairy stories?

THE AMAZING REVELATIONS OF RECENTLY DISCOVERED SCHOOLS OF ASTROLOGY

Astronomy and astrology were taken very seriously in the days of the prophets. Few kings or leaders of nations were without their court astrologer and there were schools of astrology where budding young star-gazers studied.

Little wonder that archaeological excavations have, in recent years, brought to light very extensive information about astronomical patterns stretching back many thousands of years. There is now a considerable amount of information from Chinese, Babylonian, Egyptian, Greek, Roman and Jewish sources available to the expert.

Comets were regarded as being portentious, and ancient believers in 'what the stars foretell' were able to point to the assassination of Caesar (44 B.C.) and the suicide of Nero, as being among the many events which had been preceded by awesome comets rushing through the night sky.

The Jewish rabbinic writer Abarbanel had maintained that the Messiah would appear when there was a conjunction of the stars Jupiter and Saturn. According to Jewish tradition Jupiter was thought of as the kingly star and Saturn was the protector of Israel. Saturn was regarded by some non-Jewish astrologists as being the 'god of the Jews'. Pisces was the sign of the Messiah.

In the early 1600's there lived an Imperial mathematician and Astronomer Royal, who resided in Prague. His name was Johannes Kepler. Unfortunately, apart from being a brilliant man, he was also regarded as something of a visionary and for that reason his work lost credence among this contemporaries. Kepler became a mystic when mysticism was definitely unfashionable.

On the night of December 17th, Kepler had his telescope trained on the heavens, for he knew that an exceptional event was to take place: Saturn and Jupiter were to enter a conjunction in the constellation of Pisces. A 'conjunction' as far as the layman is concerned, merely means the positioning of two stars on the same degree of longtitude.

As he watched, the two stars seemed to come closer together until all he could see in the sky was ONE bright star of wonderful brilliance. Probably the awe-inspiring sight was the reason his mind leapt back to something he had read years before but had forgotten until that moment — the prophecy of the writer Abarbanel that the Messiah would appear when there was a conjunction of Saturn and Jupiter in the constellation of Pisces.

Few astronomers would have delved so deeply, but we owe it to Kepler's mystical turn of mind that he DID delve, and publish his findings, but it is also due to his mystical turn of mind that his findings were discredited and ignored.

The excited Kepler wondered about the meaning given to the two stars Jupiter and Saturn and to the constellation Pisces by the astrologers of the ancient world. Pisces 'the sign of the Messiah', Jupiter 'the Kingly star' and Saturn 'the protector of Israel'. You don't have to be a mystic for THAT to excite you, do you? But where was the Messiah? What had happened to Israel that day in 1603? Nothing!

Fortunately it is possible for astronomers to know relatively simply exactly what the sky looked like and how the stars were positioned at any given time thousands of years before. It is not a difficult thing for them to do, the result of such an investigation will not be a product of mysticism but of science, and will be scientifically accurate.

In his planetarium Kepler turned the heavens back over sixteen hundred years and checked and rechecked his calculations, and yes, he was right, exactly the same conjunction of the two stars Jupiter and Saturn had occurred in the constellation of Pisces in the years 6-7 B.C.

As I have said, Kepler was a rather odd mixture of a man, brilliant in some ways and unbelievably naive in his mysticism in other ways. His astral discovery was published but never given credence. For one thing everyone 'KNEW' that Jesus was born in A.D. 1! Consequently Kepler's findings were dismissed as a novelty, unworthy of scientific consideration but, perhaps, of interest to those with a superstitious turn of mind.

It was not until the year 1925 that a German by the name of Schnabel deciphered the records of a famous school of astrology that had existed in Babylon in ancient times, the school was the school of astrology at Sippar in Babylon. Among the veritable mine of information he found in the ancient writings was the proof for which astrologists had been waiting. Jupiter and Saturn HAD been in conjunction in the constellation of Pisces in the year 7 B.C.!

Kepler had been right, Jupiter and Saturn DID meet in Pisces three times in the year 7 B.C.

Every few years one reads of astronomers packing their telescopes, and departing for various parts of the earth to get a view of an eclipse or some such heavenly happening. The reason they travel so far, so often, is that astral happenings cannot be seen from all parts of the earth's surface. So the next step was to find out from which part of the earth's surface the conjunction of Jupiter and Saturn in the constellation of Pisces would have been visible in 7 B.C.

Mathematical calculations showed that the happening would have been especially brilliant IN THE LAND OF ISRAEL and the Mediterranean area!

THE MYSTERIOUS EVENTS OF THE YEAR 7 B.C.

The great astrological event of the year 7 B.C. was, as we have seen, the conjunction of the stars Jupiter (the star astrologers of those days knew as 'the Kingly star') and Saturn (the star known as 'the protector of Israel') in the constellation of Pisces (known among the ancient astrologers as 'the sign of the Messiah').

They had, as we have today, in ancient writ, the predictions of many ancient seers concerning the coming of a Messiah-God. The prediction of the prophet Micah 'But thóugh Bethlehem Ephratah, though thou be little among the thousands of Judah, yet out of thee shall come forth unto me that is to be ruler in Israel, whose goings forth have been from of old, from everlasting' would have been well known to them.

Thus the 'wise men', 'Magi' or 'Astrologers' would know exactly WHERE the birth of the promised Messiah-God should take place. The MESSAGE OF THE STARS was so powerful that no astrologer could ignore it — the 'Kingly star' and the 'Protector of Israel star' in the constellation of the 'Sign of the Messiah'.

At the end of February in the year 7 B.C. the ancient astronomers watched the heavens as Jupiter moved into the constellation of Pisces and towards Saturn — what was to happen was long awaited and significant. We in this twentieth century are inclined to think that what happened on that day was of interest only in and around Bethlehem but there is evidence to indicate that astrologers throughout the whole of what we now call the Middle East were on 'standby alert' for the coming of the 'expected one'. In the event the first sighting was disappointing because the brilliance of the conjunction was subdued by the light of the sun, the sun being, on that day, also in Pisces.

At daybreak on April 12th, however, the astronomers were able to get a better view of the conjunction and were undoubtedly keeping in the forefront of their minds the three words 'Israel', 'Messiah' and 'King'.

On the morning of 29th May, it is believed, the conjunction was visible for two hours and, on December 4th of 7 B.C. Jupiter and Saturn met in the constellation of Pisces for the last time.

Was anyone of importance born in 7 B.C. who could be said to fulfil the prophecies regarding the coming Messiah?

Yes, a boy born to a virgin girl by the name of Mary from Nazareth, a girl who just happened to be in the VERY PLACE the prophet had said the Messiah-King would be born 800 years before the event!

JESUS WAS NOT BORN IN A.D. 1

'But', someone will say, Jesus was born on December 25 A.D. 1'.

The fact is Jesus was NOT born in A.D. 1 nor was he born on December 25 but the day of his birth does not matter for our purpose and I see no reason to upset the traditional Christmas celebrations just because we have the day wrong. The year of his birth DOES matter however because of the astrological evidence which flows from the year of his birth.

The A.D. system of dating is inaccurate: It is a system of dating that owes little to the birth of Christ and rather more to the imagination of a Scythian monk Dionysius Exiguus who was instructed in A.D. 533 to commence a new calendar working backwards from his day to the birth of Christ. As was to be expected, he was years adrift in his reckoning.

We can deduce roughly when Jesus was born from the New Testament narrative:

> Jesus was born in Bethlehem in Judea, in the days of Herod the King. Matthew 2:1

It is a fact of history that Herod died in the year 4 B.C.

Between the birth of Jesus and the death of Herod there were several events which necessitated there being a period of years separating the two events. There was the 'slaughter of the innocents' which drove the Jesus family into Egypt. Herod dare not have mounted that until the census ordered by Caesar had been completed and such a census could not have been completed in a few months. People had to travel from far and wide to census points and the whole operation, remembering that it affected the whole Roman world, including the necessary checks which would have to be undertaken, would take several years. Thus the Bible narrative itself indicates that the birth of Jesus could not have been very much later than B.C. 7.

We can see, therefore, that what sounds like an enjoyable myth when read at Christmastime is, a fact:

> Now when Jesus was born in Bethlehem of Judea in the days of Herod the King, behold there came wise men from the east to Jerusalem, saying, Where is he that is born King of the Jews? For WE HAVE SEEN HIS STAR IN THE EAST and we have come to worship him.
>
> Matthew 2:1,2.

The words 'in the east' can be more correctly translated 'We have seen his star in the early dawn'. That is exactly when Jupiter in conjunction with Saturn did appear — as a startlingly bright, seemingly single source of light in the early dawn.

'His star' — why his star? Because Pisces was the Messianic constellation!

"Where is he that is to be born King of the Jews?' Why did they seek the King of the Jews? Because Jupiter was the 'Kingly' star and Saturn the star considered to be the protector of Israel.

Why did they go to Bethlehem? Because that is the place the prophet Micah, speaking . . . . . . years BEFORE the event had predicted the Messiah would be born!

WHY WAS HEROD TROUBLED?

> When Herod the king, had heard these things, he was troubled and all Jerusalem with him. Matthew 2:2

Why should the mighty Herod, backed by the power of all conquering Rome, be troubled by the birth of a baby in a cattle shed? Why was 'all Jerusalem' troubled with him?

As I have said stories of girls having babies by various 'gods' were not an unusual part of the credulous life of that area. In hindsight we may find it quite natural for Jesus to be born in a cattle-shed but it would have been unthinkable to Herod that the King of the Jews would be born in that way.

Flavius Josephus, the ancient Jewish historian, gives us the answer. He tells us that at the time of the birth of Jesus it was said in Jerusalem that there had been a SIGN IN THE HEAVENS proclaiming the birth of the

Jewish king.

Jerusalem at that time had a very well developed centre of astrological studies and it is evident that the significance of the conjunction had been widely rumoured, both by astrologers and by the many devout people who had studied the ancient seers.

Next Christmas when you are sitting in your chair, full of Christmas turkey and pudding, perhaps you will look for a moment at the star on top of your Christmas tree and reflect that the virgin girl of Bethlehem and her son were very mysterious people indeed!

2 History's Greatest Hoax

In floating the proposition that the Virgin Mary might have lived and died in England it is altogether proper that we should ask what kind of nation Britain was immediately prior to and during her lifetime.

It is important too, that we should know the relationship between Britain, Rome, the conquerors of Palestine, and the rest of the world at that time.

YOU CAN NEVER BELIEVE PROPAGANDA

Fortunately Adolf Hitler did not live long enough to write his 'History of the Jewish People' because had he prevailed and been able to do so people living in a time remote from our day would have had an inaccurate view of the character of European Jewry between the first and second world wars. The obscene lies Hitler's propaganda machine spewed forth about the Jews are better not repeated but two thousand years from now they could have been considered historic fact if the allies had not prevailed.

It is not unusual for the despot to malign those he seeks to conquer, what other way has he of excusing his actions and presenting himself in a good light to posterity?

History, even at it's most accurate, is usually derivative and often coloured by the opinions and prejudices of the writer. Eye witnesses, even those with good intent, as every detective knows, can be hopelessly inaccurate after the lapse of months or even weeks. Witnesses with ill-will or an 'axe to grind' can cause 'history' to be written in such a way as to be hardly recognisable as what actually happened.

When written history emanates from war propaganda then it is a foolish person indeed who gives it unqualified acceptance.

ALL war propaganda, including our own, is less than truthful, the worst of it is downright dishonest and sometimes malevolent. The Spanish have quite a different view of the history of the Spanish Armada than that which we have. The Egyptians have a different version of the Six Day War from that of the Jewish State of Israel. The Northern States of America have a different version of the rights and wrongs of the American Civil War from the Southern States. A Russian history of the past seventy years would leave most Westerners agog because of it's deliberate mistakes.

It is a fact of history, a fact that must be faced, that the more vile the oppressor the more untruthful his propaganda about the people he has subjected must be.

No more vile and monstrous tyranny has afflicted mankind than that regime which so many historians so proudly acclaim as the civilising influence on our land, PAGAN ROME.

It is so astounding a fact that it is difficult to comprehend it, but it is true none the less that British history as taught in our schools and colleges is so coloured by, as almost to be based on, Caesar's Roman war propaganda. Most history books dismiss the whole of pre-Roman British history in a few lines as if to attest to the belief that before Rome there was no meaningful nation here.

The opposite is the fact as we shall see!

THE ROMAN INVASION OF 55 B.C.

Julias Caesar's army, which had subjugated the best armies in Europe and Asia gathered at Witsand, near Calais, and on 5th August B.C. 55 crossed the narrow waters of the Channel in two divisions.

Fifty-five days later, having penetrated only seven miles inland and having experienced a military defeat of major proportions Caesar returned with his army to the comparative safety of the continent.

The second attempted invasion of Britain by the Romans commenced on May 10 in B.C. 54. That was about forty-seven years before the boy Jesus was born to the virgin in Bethlehem. Julias Caesar was again repulsed and, despite the excuses the apologists would make for his failure, we know that the invasion was a serious attempt to subjugate these islands.

It has been said that the B.C. 54 invasion was a military 'probe' or advance party, but the numbers of ships and troops were too great for that to be the case and Dion Cassius tells us that Caesar had intended to carry the war into the interior of Britain but found his forces inadequate to meet the British opposition. On this occasion Julius Caesar and his brutish band were so thoroughly trounced by the British army that Roman forces were to threaten and posture but not to return for almost a hundred years. Despite being supported by two divisions of Rome's best fighting troops Caesar was only able to penetrate some SEVENTY MILES inland against a British army which he subsequently wrote of as 'painted savages'!

On September 10, Caesar concluded a hasty and ignominious peace at

St. Albans. Just four months after it had landed, and become pinned down, on the coast of Kent, the army which had marauded at will through Europe and Asia had been stopped in it's tracks and beat a hasty retreat and headed, once again, as they had done the previous year, under cover of darkness for the comparative safety of the French coast.

In this second invasion above a thousand ships were used and five legions — Gibbons puts the number at 60,000 — disembarked. Having experienced a beating at the hands of the British in B.C. 55, and hoping that he could avoid a similar fate, Julias Caesar brought some of the best fighting men that Rome could produce to these shores for the B.C. 44 invasion.

A storm had damaged the Roman fleet and so, to pass the weary hours while his soldiers were repairing the fleet, Caesar wrote A DESCRIPTION OF THE BRITISH PEOPLE:

> 'Most of the inland inhabitants do not sow corn, but live on milk and flesh, and are clad in skins. ALL the Britons, indeed, dye themselves with wood which occasions a bluish colour, and thereby have a more terrible appearance in fight.
>
> Caesar. Gallic War. Volume 2.

It is surprising what some people can learn about ALL British people in a few weeks isn't it? And without going further inland than seventy miles!

That is the basis on which historians have, over the years, made their assumptions about the degree of civilisation existing in Britain prior to the Roman invasion. THAT is the foundation upon which has been erected the fallacious edifice of that which we are taught about ourselves: The writings of a tyrant, about a people he had hardly seen and in whose country he had only been for a few weeks during which time he had been confined within a very tight perimeter.

THE BRITISH ARMY A WORLD-CLASS FIGHTING FORCE IN B.C. 54

Morgan writes:

'To estimate aright the military abilities of Caswallon (the British leader), and the resources of the British people at this period of the first collision of our island with the continent, it should be borne in mind that they were engaged against perhaps the ablest general of antiquity, heading an army to which, either before or after the invasion, France, Spain, Western Germany, Africa, Egypt, Asia and finally Rome itself succumbed; the conquerors, in fact, of

> Europe, Asia, and Africa, and the real founders of the imperial dynasty of the Caesars. The double repulsion of the Julian expedition by the ancient Britons has never received due weight or consideration. It yet remains unparalleled in British history.'

Caesar could malign the British and call them barbarians but Caesar was never able to explain how the best fighting men Rome could produce were soundly trounced by 'painted savages' or why the armies of Rome dare not return for some ninety years.

NINETY YEARS OF THREATENED INVASION

Ninety years of tension during which invasion was constantly threatened intervened between the peace concluded at St. Albans in B.C. 54 and the coming again of the Romans in A.D. 43. There was the threatened invasion by Augustus Caesar during which Cynvelin commanded the British Fleet in the Channel. The threats of invasion went on and Tiberius Caesar succeeded Augustus. Caligula succeeded Tiberius in A.D. 37 and one of history's most amusing farces took place. R. W. Morgan describes it magnificently:

> 'The tranquility pervading the (Roman) empire instigated Caligula to renew the attempts at a conquest which the first and second Caesars had either failed to achieve, or prudently bequeathed to their successors. The character, however, of this emperor, compounded of mania and vice, left a memorable stamp of ridicule upon the whole expedition. The armies of Gaul and the Rhine rendezvoused at Boulogne. A Roman flotilla collected from the Spanish ports was moored, ostensibly prepared to embark the troops, in the Seine. The appearance however of a British fleet under Arviragus disconcerted and put an abrupt end to the enterprise, if indeed it was ever seriously meditated. Caligula, who felt morbid gratification in burlesqueing the most momentous measures of state, and scandalizing his subjects by the maddest freaks of imperial caprice, held a grand review of his splendid expeditionary force on the sands of Boulogne. At it's termination, ascending the tribunal, he expiated on the glory which had already encircled his brow as one who had led his troops like Bacchus, Hercules, and Sesostris, to the confines of the earth-surrounding ocean. He asked if such renown ought to be jeopardized by an

armed exploration of an island which NATURE ITSELF HAD REMOVED BEYOND THE POWER AND JURISDICTION OF THE GODS OF ROME, and which the campaigns of the deified Caesar had only succeeded in pointing out the wonder of the continental world. 'Let us comrades,' he continued, adopting the well known phrase of the great Julius 'leave these Britons unmolested. TO WAR BEYOND THE BOUNDS OF NATURE IS NOT COURAGE, BUT IMPIETY. Let us rather load ourselves with the bloodless spoils of the Atlantic ocean which the same beneficent goddess of nature pours on these sands so lavishly at our feet. Follow the example of your emperor — behold,' he added, suiting the action to the word, 'I wreathe for laurel this garland of green seaweed around my immortal brow, and for spolia optima I fill my helm with these smooth and brilliant shells. Decorated with these we will return to Rome, and, instead of a British king, Neptune and Nereus, the gods of ocean themselves, shall follow captives to the Capitol behind our triumphal car. To each of you, my fellow soldiers in this arduous enterprize, I promise a gratuity of a year's extra stipend in merited acknowledgment of your services and fidelity to your emperor . . . The British fleet gazed with astonishment on these bronzed and mail-clad veterans disporting themselves in the childish amusement of collecting shells on the seashore.'

When Claudius assembled his troops for the invasion of A.D. . . . he had learned well the lessons of his predecessors. One of the largest invasion fleets Rome had ever assembled appeared off the coast of England. So great a fleet was it that the British fleet retired to Torbay, being overwhelmed by the sheer weight of numbers.

THE ROMANS MUTINY IN FEAR OF THE BRITISH

Such was the reputation of the British Army, it's renown throughout Europe and such was the Roman fear of the British as a unique and effective fighting force that the Roman army mutinied saying 'We will march anywhere in the world but not out of it.'

That was the respect the soldiery of the greatest Empire in the world had for the British Army and Navy. Rather an unusual respect if we are to believe that our forebears were 'painted savages'.

Later in the campaign, as we shall see, Claudius had himself to rush to Britain with reinforcements when three of Rome's finest generals were in danger of defeat.

Can any greater hoax on history have ever been perpetrated than that which represented the British nation at the time of the coming of the Romans as being 'painted savages'?

That Caesar wrote his description of the British people from malice rather than error is to be seen by the fact that there had been British visitors to Rome long before Caeser set foot on these shores for the first time. All Rome KNEW how highly civilized the British were.

When Caesar first came here there was already a strong and well disciplined British army and navy. The British had fine roads as we know from the fact that the British were great charioteers, and one does not become skilled in the arts of the chariot without having roads on which to use them.

PRE-ROMAN BRITISH UNIVERSITIES

There was too, in Britain in those days, a system of jurisprudence which would be the envy of many a nation today. Universities abounded, existing in, among others, the towns of York, Canterbury, Winchester, St. Albans, Cambridge, Carlisle, Manchester, Colchester, Worcester, Chester, Doncaster, Warwick, Bristol, Leicester, Lincoln, Gloucester, Chichester, Cirencester, Dorchester, Carmarthen, Caernarvon, Exeter and Bath.

The studies in these places of learning were not by any means primitive including, as they did, astronomy, geometry, medicine, poetry, public speaking and philosophy. It was not by chance that Caractacus and Boedicea were able to make such majestic speeches.

One only has to read the Triads of the Druids to realise that a high degree of civilisation existed in Britain while Rome was yet pagan and governed by a cruel regime which compared in cruelty to the regimes of Hitler and Stalin.

In the Triads of Molmutius we read: 'There are three tests of Civil Liberty: Equality of rights — equality of taxation and freedom to come and go.'

Yet another of his Triads reads: 'There are three civil birthrights of every Briton: The right to go wherever he pleases — the right, wherever he is, to protection from his land and his sovereign and the right of equal privileges and equal restrictions.'

Mr. Harrison Hill has written: 'The Laws of Dunvallo Molmutius, sixteenth king of the Britons, who reigned above 400 years before the birth of Christ. These are the first published laws in Britain, and together with those of Queen Mercia, were translated by Gildas into Latin.' Quoted in Wharton's Law Lexicon.

All evidence points to the fact that, far from being the barbarians Caesar would have had us believe, the British nation was, during the life of the Virgin Mary, a highly civilized, free, learned and prosperous society.

Here in these islands mercy reigned supreme while Rome was yet enjoying the barbarism of the 'games'.

3 The Jesus Family And The Jewish National Party

It is perhaps inevitable, though not the more satisfactory for that, that Mary the mother of Jesus and Jesus himself should, having become central to one of the world's great religions, be thought of as being almost legendary characters.

Certainly it is difficult for most people to think of the Virgin Mary and Jesus as real people who lived in the real world.

So difficult has religion made it to comprehend Jesus as a real person that there has even been some debate as to whether he lived at all. No such doubts have been expressed about the historic existence of Mohammed though he lived only some six centuries after Jesus. That is the extent to which some sections of the church have made Jesus unbelievable.

How can anyone possibly appreciate the real flesh-and-blood Mary when the only thing they know, and have been permitted to know about the Virgin Mary are the altogether imaginary and unrealistic depictions of her by religious artists, and the Bible stories which most of our preachers do not take the trouble to put into any historic or geographic context?

It is almost impossible to see the traditional depictions of the Virgin Mary, the ever placid expression, the ever clean robes, the ever young and virginal face and the ever present halo without losing all realisation that this was a woman who actually lived on this planet. The religious desire to honour the Virgin Mary has resulted in her 'public image' being such as does not cause one to believe in the reality of the woman. Superstition and myth are concepts that have been writ large over the story of the mother of Jesus.

Similarly, how can anyone appreciate as a historic flesh-and-blood reality, a man who is ridiculously depicted as always standing at doors knocking, balefully waiting for someone, who never does, to open them? Jesus, too, has that ever present halo hovering above his head and the fact that he seems effeminate and always to be in danger of bursting into tears may be one of the reasons why there are far fewer men than women in many of our churches.

How can anyone believe, as a reality, in someone who is depicted as being so hygienic that his white robes, even after forty days in the wilderness, did not become dirty and look as though they had just been brought washing powder advert white and stiffly starched from the airing cupboard?

It is not showing reverence to Jesus to deny his humanity nor to present him as an unreal person whose clothes did not become dirty, whose body did not stink when he sweated and who never performed any of the natural functions of the body. It does nothing for his 'public image' to depict him forever wandering about followed by a flock of sheep. He DID say he was the good shepherd but he was speaking figuratively and he made it plain that his 'flock' was comprised of human 'sheep'. It's a pity that the very macho, very astute, international traveller Jesus has been reduced by religious art to a first century wimp.

Yet the picture religious art and writing gives of Mary and Jesus bears no resemblance to what they were really like. Joseph to whom she was espoused evidently saw no quality in her which caused him to think of her as anything other than an ordinary fifteen year old girl. No divine expression shone from her face which stopped people in their tracks, no halo danced brightly over her head, no wonderful words of prophecy or wisdom fell from her lips.

When Mary told Joseph she was pregnant he reacted as any just man of his time would have done towards any ordinary girl of his time. It was NOT incredible to him that she may have had intercourse with someone else, he does not seem to have considered the possibility that she and her medical advisers were mistaken in their diagnosis. Joseph accepted that she was pregnant and decided to put her away privately. This does not lead us to believe that there was anything about Mary which would lead anyone to think of her as being extraordinary.

It took an 'angelic' reference to her fidelity to persuade Joseph that he had not been betrayed and, as we shall see later, it is doubtful even then that he ever fully came to terms with the virgin birth.

As with Jesus it must be said that the well-laundered clothes so beloved of religious art does nothing to make us believe in the Virgin Mary as a real person. She probably did not have a 'peaches and cream' complexion (it would be quite uncharacteristic of a Jewess living in the torrid heat of Palestine) and she would have behaved as any other little girl living in Palestine at the time.

It is unfortunate that organised religionists throughout the ages have overdone the virginal image because, as we have seen, the FACTS of the incarnation are remarkable enough without being added to in an altogether unrealistic way by those who, it would seem, would feel it needful to pour scent on a rose.

MARY WAS NOT A LIFELONG VIRGIN

Mary was not, and the writers of the scriptures do not claim that she was, a lifelong virgin. Subsequent to the birth of Jesus, Mary had consistent sexual intercourse with her husband and gave birth to other children, the brothers and sisters of Jesus, in the normal way. Mary gave birth to no less than seven children. There is every reason to believe that Mary continued to have a normal sex life with her husband Joseph, with all that entailed, until he died.

Sometimes religious thinkers are inclined to assume, perhaps because they are conditioned to do so from childhood, that lifelong virginity was highly prized at the time of Mary — it was not! Nothing could be more despised than virginity within the married state. In fact St. Paul calls it 'fraud'! (1. Corinthians 7:5) A virgin was chosen as the vehicle for the birth of Jesus for that specific purpose, there was no proscription that she should subsequently remain a virgin.

The whole mistaken doctrine of Mary's perpetual virginity comes about because one part of the Christian Church has had the desire to deify her and the other has, for years, for some unknown reason, assumed that sex, even within marriage, was something to be considered 'dirty' and the womb that had born a child unclean.

A thorough reading of the Bible, both Old and New Testaments, will show that sexual intercourse within marriage was considered to be not only an honourable thing but a duty which brought nothing but respect to both partners. That is as we would expect, how could it be otherwise when God Himself commanded man to 'multiply'? Do YOU know of any other way of doing that than by having sex?

Yes, Mary, to all physical appearance, was an ordinary woman, she would not have been seen to be exceptional when seen in a crowd, there is no record of the Blessed Virgin being mobbed despite the angelic furore at the nativity. She lived a normal marital sex life, she had to perform ALL the personal ablutions that other women have to perform and, when she travelled in the heat of the day, she became dirty and smelly. It is this REAL woman not the Mary of paint and plaster of Paris who was the mother of Jesus.

Until we come to a realisation of how 'normal' Jesus and his mother were, ordinary people will, though paying lip service to a belief in them, continue to think of Jesus and Mary more as myths of the ilk of George and the Dragon than real people.

THE JESUS FAMILY AND THEIR LIFESTYLE

It is surprising how the myth of the poorness of the Jesus family gained credence from the earliest days of the history of Christianity. It is a story which, politically has something in it for every shade of opinion. The rich were quick to see that the poor could be made to accept their lot more easily if they thought they were less worse off than the Son of God and his mother. They were inclined to feel less antagonism towards the well-off and privileged when they were made to believe that God had worked through a 'poor girl' who probably had too little to eat and too few clothes just like their wives and daughters. At least, they would reason, their children had not been born in a 'cattle-shed'. The poverty of Mary and Jesus was a very convenient doctrine and made many millions of people satisfied with their earthly lot who would not otherwise have been satisfied with it.

Socialism too, found comfort in the story of the 'poor' Mary and her child. Did it not show the heights to which the poor could aspire? Was not the story of Jesus also the story of one man's battle against poverty and the establishment? Was Jesus not the original 'angry young man'?

Sadly the Jesus story has been used to prop up many 'isms both religious and political and the real message ignored. The REAL message of Jesus was that ALL establishments become corrupt and truth is capable of residing and surviving only in the individual. He regarded 'isms as being subject to a constant pattern of generation, degeneration and regeneration.

Still it does make the 'Mary story' a little more romantic and, perhaps, a little more socialist to say that Mary was poor but there is no evidence for such an assertion. All the evidence would point to her being a person perhaps of royal descent and certainly of some influence if not of actual personal wealth.

MARY STAYED AT HOTELS WHEN SHE TRAVELLED

I will come later to the traditions that the rich shipowner, metal merchant and Minister for Mines of the Roman Empire, Joseph of Arimathea, was her uncle, but even without that being a fact there are stong indications that Mary was not poor.

Inevitably I will be pointed to the fact that Jesus was born of Mary in a manger. Preachers love that part of the Christmas story, they speak as though there is some inherent virtue in poverty, which there is not. Poverty is certainly undesirable, a misfortune and a pity but NEVER a virtue!

We are told that Jesus was born in a manger because 'there was NO ROOM at the inn', Inn keepers were no different from their modern hotel keeping counterparts, prices varied 'according to season' and we can be sure that the census of Augustus Caesar would be considered a 'high season'. Not everyone could AFFORD to stay at an inn, especially when they were charging the inflated prices they charged when there were a lot of people about.

It would seem that Mary and Joseph COULD afford to stay at the inn, had tried to book a room, but found the hotel was full. That does not indicate poverty, quite the contrary, it would indicate that Mary and Joseph were intent on staying at the inn had there been room. If that is not so then the statement that 'there was no room at the inn' becomes superfluous.

JOSEPH WAS A WELL-PAID ARTISAN

The 'poor' carpenter image granted to Joseph is no more accurate than that of the 'poor' babe in the manger. We should not judge the income of carpenters in Joseph's time as being the same as that of a carpenter in the past two hundred or so years. The fact is that carpenters in Joseph's day were skilled artisans — they were certainly NOT poor.

In days when there was no machinery to produce things made of wood, the carpenter was a very important, and a very skilled person. Then, as now, it was not often skilled people sold their skills cheaply. The word 'carpenter' is a contraction of the word 'cartpenter' literally 'one who makes carts' Joseph would have had a thriving business making ploughs, yokes, saddles and goads.

We shall see that at no time during the life of Jesus did he live a life of poverty. He was certainly no poor wandering preacher. Even at the end of his life we are told that the Roman soldiers 'cast lots for his robe' because that robe was 'seamless' or broadloom. A seamless robe was the 'Saville Row' standard of dress of New Testament days! A garment as indicative of wealth in Jesus' day as a mink coat today.

THE JESUS CLAN

We have the view of Jesus that he lived in Nazareth until he was about thirty and then, one day, walked out of the house and began to preach. That view is, as we shall see, quite fallacious.

Having suddenly decided to preach, we are given the impression that Jesus became some kind of Pied Piper of Palestine, that a number of people who did not know Jesus were so impressed with his teaching that they followed him. That too is a fallacy!

The first followers, at the beginning the only, and always the closest followers of Jesus were his family, his affluent friends and their business acquaintances. Often we get the idea that Jesus walked the shores of Galilee muttering 'follow me' to people who were not known to him but that is not the case as we shall see.

The Virgin Mary was the sister of Mary Cleophas and Mary Cleophas was the wife of the Virgin Mary's husband, Joseph's brother (according to Hegesippus and John 19:25).

We know the story well of how a wilderness preacher by the name of John the Baptist proclaimed the coming of the Messiah and later baptised Jesus in the River Jordan. Even John the Baptist was 'family'. Elizabeth, mother of John the Baptist, was the Virgin Mary's second cousin.

Mary Salome, mother of the disciples James and John (Zebedee), was also a second cousin to Mary.

So we see that the Virgin Mary, Joseph her husband, Jesus, John the Baptist and his mother, the disciples James and John and their parents were all of the same family.

Two others who became disciples of Jesus, Andrew and John, were friends of the family through John the Baptist.

The family had it's problems. Joseph husband of the Virgin Mary died when Jesus was quite young. Though the man was head of the house in the society of his day we do not read of Joseph after Jesus was twelve years of age, had he lived he would most certainly have accompanied Mary wherever she went and have been conspicuous at the recorded events of Jesus' life.

John the Baptist was, as everyone knows, beheaded, and his father, Zacharias, was assassinated between the temple and the altar for proclaiming the Miraculous Conception of Jesus. John's mother died before he started his ministry.

THE 'SIMPLE' FISHERMEN OF GALILEE MYTH

Zebedee, husband of Mary Zebedee, second cousin of the Virgin Mary and father of disciples James and John was a partner, with his sons, in a fishing fleet which operated on the Sea of Galilee. Who were the other partners, partners who became followers of cousin Jesus? None other than Andrew and Peter the 'poor simple fishermen' so beloved of the preacher! The fact is they were not 'poor' and they were not 'simple', between them they owned at least two, and probably more, quite large ships and were wealthy enough to have servants on the ships. Mark tells us 'they left their father Zebedee in the ship with THE HIRED SERVANTS and went after him (Jesus)'.

The large ships of the partnership undertook long journeys, fished by night and had sleeping quarters on board. It is very probable that the Zebedees, Andrew and Peter did most of the fishing in the area, an activity which obviously produced enough money for them to have servants aboard their fishing fleet.

Andrew, Peter, James and John had friends, Philip and Nathaniel and they too became disciples of Jesus.

When Jesus heard that John the Baptist had been betrayed he and Mary moved from Nazareth into Capernaum to be near the Zebedees and their friends.

WINING AND DINING IN CAPERNAUM

In Capernaum life was very different from the little town of Nazareth. Capernaum was, in the time of Jesus a busy, picturesque and important city. Excavations have attested to the fact that it was an area of extensive development. The business people of the town lived a life of gaiety, parties, drinking, eating and dancing.

At Capernaum Jesus and Mary mixed with the affluent Zebedees, the Governor and the publicans (to be more precise the revenue officials) and wined and dined at the extensive house of Matthew the revenue officer who had become converted and seems to have celebrated his conversion by throwing a party. There is the record of at least one party of considerable size that took place at Matthew's house.

That there were many others is beyond doubt for during the time of the one year of his ministry Jesus had managed to get himself the reputation of being a glutton and a winebibber. He did not deny the charge that he visited the houses of 'publicans and sinners' nor the charge that he himself drank wine and ate rather a lot. There were plenty of miracles he could have performed rather than turning water into wine had he wished to do so. He could have, for example, at the beginning of the party, turned the wine into water. It would have shown his power just as much, it would have been just as much a miracle and it would have provided a far stronger platform for the total abstentionists among us.

Jesus chose to turn the water into wine! Those at the feast had already drunk everything that was in the building and, at a wedding feast of that kind, wine would not have been in short supply. Yet here we have Jesus, often presented to us today as a 'Po-faced total abstainer', providing yet more wine for people who had already drunk their fill. Jesus must have been a lot of fun to be with! They'd have loved him in the Rugby Club at Cwmtooch!

It would seem there was no shortage of either money or revelry among the band of followers at Capernaum!

THE JERUSALEM FOLLOWERS

That Jesus was no 'simple' carpenter but a man with great debating ability, is clear from the way he debated with the intelligensia among the Jews and Romans.

Someone will make the point that he was God incarnate, and that tenant of faith we hold dear, but we are asked to believe too that he was truly man and what is under discussion now is the breadth and depth of his knowledge NOT it's source.

The Roman Centurion was forced to confess 'Never man spake like this man'. The hierachy of the Jewish faith, themselves no mean tricksters in debate, were constantly confounded by his knowledge and reparteé and at the last dared not ask him any more questions.

Soon Jesus was, as he had done in Galilee, gathering the rich and intelligent around him. There was the physician of Cyrene Dr. Luke, the entrepreneurial Joseph of Arimathea and the wealthy Mark.

Fortunately the house which was owned by the disciple Mark's parents still stands in Jerusalem. Little of Jerusalem escaped the destruction brought about by the Roman army of Titus in 70 A.D. Perhaps the only authentic building is that large house belonging to Mark's family, in the dining room of which the Last Supper was held. It was this house too which was the scene of the happenings in the 'Upper Room' on the Day of Pentecost. Anyone visiting the house even now will detect that it was a house of some substance and the dwelling of wealthy people. It was, at the time of Jesus, such an extensive house that it is probable that it was in the courtyard Peter addressed the large audience when 120 converts came to the faith.

That Jesus attracted the rich and intelligent is beyond doubt for in addition to those we have mentioned there is the 'rich young ruler' the 'ruler of the Jews'. One can imagine that wherever Jesus dwelt the air buzzed with good conversation and informed opinion.

THE VIRGIN MARY WAS NO 'COUNTRY BUMPKIN'

The Virgin Mary was not a simple, innocent, unaware small town Jewish girl. She was used to rubbing shoulders with the wealthy, hearing the earthy language of fishing tycoons, attending parties, singing, dancing, drinking wine and definitely NOT looking 'puddin' faced' as she does in the paintings of her.

She would know too about lands beyond the sea for, the Governor of Capernaum, with whom the Jesus family dined, was Roman and her uncle, Joseph of Arimathea, would tell her of his travels to Britain and probably discuss the commodity and shipping markets with her.

Some may think all that to be a flight of the imagination but it is not. Is it reasonable to think that after the defeat of the Roman armies in Britain in B.C. 55 and B.C. 54 the Romans would not discuss our land wherever they went in the world? Many of the Roman officers and men who fought in the British and European campaigns and the sons of men that had fought in this part of the world would have subsequently seen service in Palestine and told their warrior stories. The Roman Empire depended on the British Isles for the tin, without which their armies could not have functioned as effectively as they did. Is it reasonable to suppose that conversation over dinner did not involve many a story of these Islands?

Nor is it imagination to write of the social life of Jesus and Mary. As we have mentioned, Jesus himself tells us that he had been called a 'winebibber and a glutton' (Luke 7:34) and, though I am sure he neither ate nor drank to excess, he must have drunk considerable amounts of wine (after all the water was unsafe and wine was the national drink) and eaten with great pleasure to have been called that — and he didn't deny it!

One can only stand amazed at the tunnel vision of those who would have us believe that wine was non-alcoholic in those days but then there ARE still people who believe the earth is flat!

Feasts such as Matthew held in his house were far from being either of a kin with Sunday school treats nor were they solemn affairs and we know that at least one, Peter, among the fishermen was not averse to cussing, even after his conversion (Mark 14:71). There would be eating, discussion of topics of the day, singing, dancing, story telling, laughter and drinking and all would join in.

The Romans apart, would not the seafarers talk about Britain at those parties? Joseph of Arimathea would have done so to be sure but is it conceivable that the seafarers, Caesar had written his 'Gallic War' years before, would not have told of the island in the Atlantic beyond the Columns of Hercules which Caesar had visited?

Is it conceivable that none of the crews of the Phoenician ships which brought tin from the mines of Cornwall to Palestine would have mentioned Britain, especially as the Phoenicians had been trading between Cornwall and the Middle East since the days when King Solomon needed tin for the construction of his temple? There was certainly at that time a considerable knowledge of Rome, the islands of the Mediterranean, France, Gaul and Spain.

Perhaps we only find the proposition that the Virgin Mary came to Britain so surprising because we have an altogether fallacious view of the kind of person she was, because, as we have said, we have never thought about her as a real, living, flesh-and-blood human being.

Neither have we thought of Jesus as being a real person who lived in the real world. We have not thought of the kind of society in which she and Jesus lived and have regarded Palestine as being a land in isolation.

When we appreciate the fact that there was considerable intercourse between the British Isles and the Middle East in those days both by reason of commerce, the tin trade, and because of the world-wide political influence of Rome, we find the proposition that either Jesus or Mary, or both of them, visited the British Isles less surprising.

THE MYSTERY OF THE MISSING YEARS

The Jesus family moved to Capernaum when he was about thirty-nine years of age, soon after he had been baptised by his cousin John the Baptist in the River Jordan.

There is no record, in the Bible, of what happened to Mary and Jesus between the time Jesus was twelve years of age and the time he was thirty-nine years of age.

Is it not surprising that, if Jesus and Mary lived in Palestine during those 'missing years', this close knit family did not keep a record of his activities in the Holy Land? They kept a record of what he said when he was twelve years of age and they kept a record of his sayings when he was thirty-nine years of age but they don't report anything he said or did between those ages — why? Can we really believe that he neither said nor did anything of importance for twenty-seven years?

Could it be that either Mary or Jesus or both of them were not in Palestine? It seems the only reasonable assumption as we shall see in our next chapter.

4 The Mystery of Jesus' Missing Years

There is an assumption that Jesus lived the whole of his life in Palestine, it is an assumption which few people would ever challenge. Yet there is not one shred of evidence for such an assumption. On the contrary there is considerable evidence to suggest that Jesus DID NOT live in Palestine for very long during the forty or so years of his life.

Come with me for a moment to the banks of the River Jordan about the year A.D. 33.

John the Baptist who was the self-confessed forerunner of the Messiah was reaching the climax of his 'desert prophet' ministry. You will remember that he was the cousin of Jesus and the two families had been very close at the time of the birth of both the children. In the normal course of events they would have been brought up together, attending as the Jews did, the three great feasts of the faith.

On this occasion John is preaching his gospel of repentance and baptising people in the muddy waters of the river.

Suddenly he looks up at a man standing among the thronging crowd on the bank of the river. The crowd becomes hushed as John's gaze is rivetted on the face of the stranger and then John speaks to the crowd and says 'Behold the lamb of God which taketh away the sins of the world'.

It is a strange phrase to us today, though our forebears would have understood it well, the old time revivalists made it familiar, through their hymns with 'Are you washed in the soul cleansing blood of The Lamb?'

The Jews standing on the banks of the Jordan that day would realise it's meaning too, for they would relate it to many an instance in their own history, many a part of their own liturgy and the thin red thread of substitutional death which ran through their scriptures — the books we now call The Old Testament.

Their minds would go back to the early Genesis story of the Garden of Eden and they would remember that, after the fall of man, Adam and Eve Perceived that they were naked. Their religion knew the great symbolism of the necessary death of the animal from which, it was said, God had made coats of skins for Adam and Eve and they would imagine Adam looking at the animal and saying 'He died for me'.

It is strange that religious art has chosen to show Adam and Eve covering their nakedness with leaves. Perhaps religious artists have done so because they think that is the sensible thing for God to have done. Indeed they would be right in thinking it as easy to cover Adam and Eve with a covering of plaited grass or wool as to give them 'coats of skin', especially in a hot climate and it would certainly have been more humane.

There is a symbolism however to the coats of skin, a symbolism which would come into the mind of each Jew who heard John the Baptist's words on that day. It was a symbolism based upon the saying 'For without the shedding of blood, there is no remission of sin'.

John's hearers would think too of a later incident in their history, the time of the testing of Abraham which had brought forth from their God the first of the great promises which, they conceived, made them the chosen people. It was the incident in which Abraham had been asked by God to sacrifice his son upon the altar.

They would remember how Abraham had taken Isaac to the place of sacrifice and Isaac with deep trust in his father had, in a supreme moment of pathos, asked 'But father, where is the lamb?' to which Abraham had replied 'God will provide a lamb'. As Abraham raised the sacrificial knife over his son's body he saw a ram caught in the thicket and took it as God's provision to save Isaac from death.

The story was one which rarely failed to bring tears to Jewish eyes. As they heard John's words they would imagine Isaac looking at the dead ram and saying 'He died for me'.

Their minds would go back to that ominous night in Egypt when their forefathers had been warned that the angel of death was to smite all the first-born of the land. All their lives, each year at the Passover, they celebrated that night before their nation's coming out of Egypt and recalled the warning. It was an incident never far from their minds. The warning had been accompanied by a promise that those who sprinkled 'the blood' on the lintels of their houses would be saved. They would imagine the Israelites emerging from their homes the following morning while the Egyptians were burying their dead and remembering their sacrificial lambs with the words 'He died for me'.

The progression was natural to them; in the case of Isaac, a lamb for an individual; in the case of the passover a lamb for a family; in the case of the Temple sacrifice a lamb for a nation and now, on the banks of the Jordan, John the Baptist heralding the Messiah and developing the age old theme of substitutional death or as our theologians like to express it, vicarious sacrifice, and proclaiming A LAMB FOR THE WORLD!

One can imagine how, with their religious background and understanding of the teaching of vicarious sacrifice ('He died for me'), they would thrill to the words John spoke.

The story of Jesus' baptism is well known, of how the Holy Spirit descended on him in the form of a dove and how the voice from heaven proclaimed 'This is my beloved son in whom I am well pleased'.

HOW DO YOU FORGET A VIRGIN BIRTH?

Now let me emphasise again the fact that John the Baptist was the cousin of Jesus and the fact that his father, Zacharias had been assassinated for proclaiming the miraculous conception of Jesus.

Put together with those facts the closeness of Jewish families. Their religious life and observances ensured that families kept in close contact with one another.

Think back to the day of Jesus' birth and the family stories that would be told about the day Elizabeth, John's mother, was told of Mary's pregnancy and was so excited 'the babe leapt in her womb'.

We can imagine how, at the three obligatory feasts of the Jewish faith they would have met and how the family would look with awe upon the lad Jesus who had been born among so many miraculous happenings. He would obviously have been the centre of attention and there would have been no possibility of him being forgotten. The families would have loved to recall the events of his birth, how the wise men had brought gifts of gold, frankincense and myrrh, how the angel's message had sounded through the night air to the shepherds as they watched their flocks in the fields.

Think of the family tears that would be shed as they remembered the thousands of children slaughtered by Herod as he sought the baby Jesus. NOT THINGS A FAMILY WOULD EASILY FORGET!

Yet, though John had had revealed to him that the man standing on the bank of the river was 'the lamb of God' who was destined to take away the sin of the world, he did NOT RECOGNISE HIM as cousin Jesus!

Later, when John was in prison, he sent his disciples to enquire of the man he had baptised 'Art though he that should come, or do we look for another?'

> 'And it came to pass when Jesus had ceased commanding his disciples, he departed from there to teach and to preach in their cities.
> Now, when John had heard in prison of the works of Christ, he sent two of his disciples, and said unto him, Art thou he that should come, or do we look for another?'

John knew only too well from the events of the advent day that JESUS was the promised Messiah. The wise men had affirmed it, the herald angels had proclaimed it and Herod had feared it. Zacharias, John's father, a priest, had been assassinated for saying so. Obviously then, what John DID NOT know was that the man he had baptised was Jesus.

Why did John not recognise Jesus? In the normal course of events, as a family, they would have spent a lot of time worshipping together. The only plausible answer would seem to be because he had not seen Jesus since Jesus was twelve.

John had been preaching for several years, why had he not baptised Jesus before? Perhaps because Jesus had not been to one of his meetings before and one of the reasons for that could be that he was not in the land between the age of twelve and the age of thirty-nine.

THE STRANGER TAX

> 'And when they were come to Capernaum, they that collected tribute money came to Peter, and said, Does not your master pay tribute? he said, Yes. And when he had come into the house, Jesus spoke first to him, saying. What do you think, Simon? Of whom do the kings of the earth take custom or tribute? Of their own children or STRANGERS?
> Peter said unto him, Of strangers.'

Note the phrase 'Of whom do the KINGS OF THE EARTH take custom or tribute?' It is not unusual for theologians to say that Jesus was being asked to pay the Temple tax but that is not so. There were two taxes levied one was the Temple tax and the other the 'Stranger tax'.

What was being asked of Jesus was NOT the temple tribute but the tribute levied by Rome on all who were foreigners in Capernaum. Notice carefully that Jesus made it plain whose head was on the coin in which he was being asked to pay. He said 'Render unto Caesar that which is Caesar's and unto God that which is God's'. The coin in which Jesus paid the tax was Roman and IT WAS FORBIDDEN TO PAY THE TEMPLE TAX IN A FOREIGN COINAGE.

Why was he asked to pay the tax? The Romans, though a cruel race, were scrupulously fair in administering their taxes. There can only be one reason he was asked to pay the tax and that is that Jesus had not been in Palestine for some years. You will notice how readily the disciples agreed that Jesus DID pay the tax. Why did Jesus pay the stranger tax? Because he invariably conformed with the law and it was the law that he should pay because he had not been in the land FOR A NUMBER OF YEARS.

In the first chapter of the Gospel of John, verses 45-48 there is a story which is strange indeed if Jesus had not been absent from Palestine. Before reading the quotation it is necessary to understand that Nathanael lived in Cana, a town just five miles from Nazareth. Again I must point my reader to the fact that all Jewish families met AT LEAST three times a year at the three obligatory feasts.

> 'Philip findeth Nathanael, and said to him, We have found him, of whom Moses in the law, and the prophets, did write, Jesus of Nazareth, the son of Joseph. And Nathanael said to him, Can there any good thing come out of Nazareth? Philip saith to him, Come and see. Jesus saw Nathanael coming to him, and said of him, Behold an Israelite indeed, in whom is no guile! Nathanael said to him, How do you know me? Jesus answered and said to him, Before that Philip called you, when you were under the fig tree, I saw you.'

Is it not strange that, if Jesus had lived in Palestine continuously, Nathanael did not know him? Jesus had said to Mary when he was twelve 'Don't you understand that I should be about my Father's business?' If he was about his father's business at the age of twelve, are we to believe that between the ages of twelve and thirty-nine he ceased being about his father's business? On the other hand, if he WAS about his Father's business from childhood to the age of thirty-eight then why did Nathanael not know who this man who claimed to be the Messiah was? Such a message could not have gone unnoticed in a rural community such as existed in Nazareth and Cana at the time.

Another telling passage is to be found in Matthew chapter 13 verses 54-57. Ferrar Fenton in his translation makes the point clearly but the reader may if he wishes compare the Authorised Version and find that there is no essential difference in the meaning of the two translations.

> 'And coming into His own country, He (Jesus) taught them in their synagogue; and so greatly astonished were they that they asked "WHERE has this man acquired his knowledge and power? Is he not the son of that carpenter? Is not His mother called Mary, and His brothers, James, Joseph, Simon and Judah? And His sisters, are they not all here with us? WHERE then did he attain all this?

Evidently even the synagogue authorities at the synagogue in which the family would have continually worshipped, though they knew Jesus' father, his mother and his brothers and sisters did not know where Jesus had received his education. That is an impossibility in such a close community, if Jesus had been educated in Palestine.

Jesus himself, in fact, confirmed he had not been in Palestine when he replied to them 'A prophet is not without honour, except in his own country'.

There is yet another and more profound reason for us to believe that Jesus was not in Palestine those years between the age of twelve and the age of thirty-nine but that is a long story and I will deal with it in another chapter.

5 The British Royal Family's Blood Relationship to The Virgin Mary

As we have seen it is easy to think of Palestine in Mary's day as being remote, even cut off, from the civilised world. To suggest that Britain was known to Jesus or the disciples of Jesus is to invite a puzzled if not mocking smile. The traditional Christian view seems not to extend, to the west of Palestine, beyond Rome.

Though everyone knows that Palestine was occupied by the forces of Rome few realise the intercourse which took place between the Middle East, Rome and Britain in those days. Still fewer have absorbed an appreciation of the amount of communication there was between nations east and west in the last century B.C. and the first century A.D.

Until we have an appreciation of how well travelled the influential people of those days were we will not have an appreciation of the real situation which existed in, what we now call, the Middle East at that time.

It is unfortunate that very little that we learn in our churches helps us relate Mary, Jesus, the disciples, any of the characters we find in the New Testament or the Roman hierarchy to the interrelated world society which existed then or to comprehend them moving across the stage of history.

That Peter was the first Bishop of Rome is believed by Roman Catholics as a matter of dogma but it is to be wondered whether it is believed as a matter of fact. St. Peter too, has been reduced by church teaching to almost a myth, a lucky mascot and someone who is the butt of jokes about heaven. His bishopric of Rome is believed hardly at all by those of the Protestant persuasion, some of whom will ignore any evidence contrary to their set view on the matter, thinking, it would seem, that a fact ignored is a fact abrogated. Yet there is little doubt that St. Peter WAS the first Jewish Bishop of Rome though NOT the first bishop of the Roman Catholic Church.

A BRITISH 'ROYAL' THE FIRST BISHOP OF ROME

The first Bishop of Rome was, in fact, a member of the British Royal

Family, Linus by name and he was succeeded by Peter who was Bishop of the Jewish Christian congregation in Rome and Paul who became the first Bishop of the Gentile Christian congregation in Rome.

For me to write of 'Jewish Christians' may seem odd to some but it should be realised that Jesus did NOT establish a religion called 'Christianity' nor did he attend a church called a 'Christian Church'. He did not see himself as founding a new religion, he did not want Jews to become Christians. Jesus wanted Jews to accept the truth that their Messiah had come — quite a different proposition. Jesus saw his ministry as being a continuation of the ministry of the Old Testament prophets but with the 'spirit' taking the place of the 'letter' and his own once-and-for-all sacrifice taking the place of the traditional sacrifices.

We know that both Peter and Paul ministered in Rome and we know that Paul was friendly with at least one British Princess, he mentions her and her husband by name in his Epistle to the Romans.

If then, Paul ministered in Rome and met British royalty in Rome and if Peter ministered in Rome, why should the thought that Mary or Jesus or both of them visited Britain be received with a rather derogatory, if polite, smile?

It was not, at the time of Jesus, as we shall see, at all uncommon for people from the Middle East to visit Britain. They had been doing it in their thousands for hundreds of years before the Virgin Mary was born! It is history's warped view of the isolation of the British Isles at that time which makes the Divine visit to Britain seem so incredible to us.

In fact the traffic was not all one way, tradition has it that Anna, Mary's mother came from Cornwall and had undertaken the journey in the opposite direction.

The main stumbling block, I think, is that most people do not think of Bible people, Mary, Jesus, Joseph of Arimathea, Pilate, Herod, the disciples and Paul as world travellers. Mentally they think of people of Bible times as being chained to their main moment in history. Thus we are inclined not to think of Pilate in any other context than standing on the balcony on that fateful day, washing his hands. We do not see him as a baby needing nappies changed, we do not see him playing games with boys in the street, we do not see him in his first sexual encounter with a woman, we do not see him with toothache. Pilate and all the Bible people are to most people disembodied concepts and we see them confined within their historic moment or moments.

If there is one thing that organised religion, of most brand names, has succeeded in doing it is to make the very real people we read of in the New Testament into almost mythological figures as cardboard and cutout as those brightly coloured sheets of nativity figures they used to give us in Sunday School.

Yet secular history is not at all silent about them and legend is fertile with accounts of their exploits, travels and their relationships. History tells us a lot about how those people lived and travelled.

THE FAMILY TREE OF JESUS

It is not generally known but there is a family tree of Jesus from the time of Adam, in the Herald's Office at the English College of Arms.

From that document we glean the information that Ann, mother of the Virgin Mary, was married three times. Her first husband was Joachim by whom she had the Virgin Mary, her second husband was Cleophas and her third Salome.

It would seem Ann liked the name Mary for in addition to the Virgin Mary she named daughter by her two other husbands 'Mary' also.

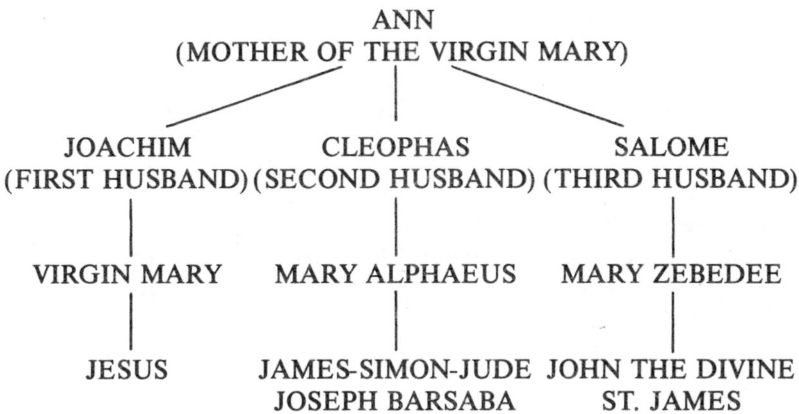

Ann had a sister by the name of Bianca who was the mother of St. Joseph. Thus St. Joseph, the Virgin Mary's husband, was also her first cousin.

That is an important fact in the development of our enquiry because it would indicate that Joseph of Arimathea was a cousin of both Mary and Joseph.

BIANCA
(AUNT OF THE VIRGIN MARY)

JOSEPH (HUSBAND OF MARY) — ELIZABETH

JESUS — JOHN THE BAPTIST

This view is confirmed in the Harl. MSS. which is held in the British Museum.

It will come as a surprise to many to realise that, far from being confined to Palestine, the Holy Family seem, through the Virgin Mary's uncle, Joseph of Arimathea, to have intermarried into British royalty and to have left Palestine to live in Britain.

THE VIRGIN MARY'S EXILE IN ENGLAND A CAREFULLY LAID PLAN

Some have assumed that the Virgin Mary's exile in England was brought about by a forced exodus from the Holy Land but there is evidence that both Jesus and Joseph of Arimathea had planned for a life in Britain for the family from the time Jesus was quite young. It would seem that the forced exodus after the resurrection of Jesus was a pre-empting of an already carefully laid plan.

A RELATIVE OF THE VIRGIN MARY MARRIES INTO THE BRITISH ROYAL FAMILY

Confirmation that Penardin, granddaughter of Joseph of Arimathea, married King Lear of Britain is to be found in a manuscript which is held at Jesus College.

o

- ANN
  - VIRGIN MARY
    - JESUS
- BIANCA
  - ELIZABETH
    - JOHN THE BAPTIST
- JOSEPH OF ARIMATHEA (UNCLE OF THE VIRGIN MARY AND JOSEPH)
  - ANNA
    - PENARDIN (MARRIED BRITISH KING LEAR)
      - BRAN (BRITISH KING)
        - CARACTACUS (BRITISH KING)
          - GLADYS (BRITISH PRINCESS WHO MARRIED ROMAN NOBLEMAN RUFUS PUDENS AND CHANGED HER NAME TO CLAUDIA AND BECAME HOST TO THE APOSTLE PAUL)

It is interesting to note that King Arthur and ALL the knights of the round table claimed descent from Joseph of Arimathea.

The above genealogies are important because they give an altogether different perspective of the interrelationship of the nations at the time of Jesus. Then, as now, it would seem that the rich, influential and famous knew each other and had far more in common than we would at first think.

A granddaughter of Joseph of Arimathea, cousin of the Virgin Mary, marries a member of the British Royal Family; a member of the British Royal Family marries a Roman commander; an Apostle of Jesus is entertained by a British Princess in Rome; a member of the British Royal Family is the first Bishop of Rome. It throws a different perspective on the world at that time — doesn't it?

6 The Great Persecution

At the very beginning of the story of Jesus' life we are told that King Herod was troubled. It was to be the pattern for Jesus' career, he continued to trouble people, especially those in authority, for the rest of his life.

Jesus troubled people after his death too, and, as we shall see in this chapter it was not a superficial sort of worry that afflicted them but a deep fear which bred an almost psychopathic antipathy. It was a fear and antipathy deep enough for them to risk their political careers to erase his memory from the thoughts of their fellow countrymen and deep enough to cause the Sanhedrin to do something no one would have dreamed it would ever do — break it's own laws and the laws of Rome.

We must take note of the depth of this fear and antipathy for it tells a story indirectly which no piece of history could ever tell. Actions speak louder than words they say and I think we all know that to be true. It is certainly true that what happened to the people who were in direct contact with Jesus and his teaching during his life, and how they reacted to him, tells us far more than the bald statements of historic record.

We have asked the question: Why was Herod King of Judea afraid of the babe born in a manger? We have seen that it was because he was born at a time and a place which had been predicted as being the time and place of the birth of the Messiah/God/King hundreds of years before.

Herod would undoubtedly have ignored the protestations of virginity made by the child's mother, not unusual claims at the time as we have seen. He would also have ignored the stories about 'Herald Angels' for credulity of such things abounded and stories of visitations by angelic beings were not at all uncommon.

He was afraid because he saw ancient predictions of the most specific kind coming to pass before his eyes, and, with the shrewdness which was Herod, recognised that a very important and unique thing had happened in Bethlehem that day.

Herod would undoubtedly have been influenced in his fear by the students of the prophets who were expecting the Messiah that very year because Daniel (700 B.C.) had given the precise date of the birth of the Messiah.

The students of astrology, there were foundations of astrology in both Babylon and Jerusalem, many of whom were NOT Israelites, had added their weight to the predictions of the prophets by predicting the mysterious conjunction of stars which, they said, would immediately precede the birth of the Messiah.

The whole of the Middle East was in ferment at the prospect of the coming of the Messiah in the days prior to the birth of Jesus.

All this added up to the babe of Bethlehem being a very unusual person indeed. Perhaps one of the most significant things about the coming of the Messiah, when he came, was that few of those steeped in religion believed he had come. Perhaps they had believed in the THEORY of the coming of the Messiah for so long that they did not really believe it would happen as a matter of fact. We can all get so used to the things we believe that they pass out of the area of vital realisation in our lives.

HEROD REALLY DID BELIEVE

Recognition of the character of Jesus seems to have been largely confined to those whose interests lay outside the realms of the established religion of their day. Hurtful as it may be to some Christians it must be said that in that respect things have not changed much.

Herod would seem to have believed in the identity of Jesus with a far greater fervour than most Christians and some Bishops do today! The coming of Jesus certainly caused Herod to ACT which is more than can be said for his impact on many of his professed followers today.

One only has to read the gospel narratives to see how deeply Jesus affected almost everyone who came into contact with him. Few could be indifferent to him, fewer still followed him and many were virulently antagonistic to him.

Our subject is not of course Jesus, except insofar as his life, death and resurrection affect his mother Mary but what happened to Jesus those last fateful days before his crucifixion, what happened to him at and after his resurrection and what happened to the earliest Christians in the days immediately following his ascension are ALL very important to our subject.

The experience of Herod was the experience of so many in the Jewish hierarchy of the time, they saw Jesus as a threat and they saw the followers of Christ as a threat. They hated the followers of the way with an almost insane hatred, a hatred that led them into behaviour of which they would not have dreamed they were capable.

Treachery is not something of which the Jewish faith either at the time of

Christ or now is particularly proud, nor, to their credit, has subterfuge played a great part in the history of that nation and yet some of their most influential leaders behaved in an almost Gestapo like manner and connived not only in sending the man of Galilee to his death but also in attempting to subsequently eradicate every trace of him from the pages of history. As we shall see, the length to which they went ot silence him was out of all proportion to the threat he would seem to have posed.

THE 'ILLEGALITIES' WHICH BROUGHT JESUS TO TRIAL

Most of the fracas between Jesus and the Pharisees were about the keeping of the law. To the Pharisees the law had become an end in itself and perhaps their attitude and the attitude of Jesus to the law is best summed up in his saying 'The Sabbath is made for man and not man for the Sabbath'.

Rarely, if ever, would the Sanhedrin countenance a miscarriage of justice. Yet it would seem that in their dealings with Jesus they went almost berserk, overthrowing all their principles of justice.

Their connivance with the treacherous Judas is surprising. There was no need for them to pay the considerable amount of blood money they did pay to Judas. Jesus was not in hiding and he was known well enough to the authorities.

The sole function of Judas was to fulfil the requirement of the law that there must be a civilian identification of an arrested person. It seems hysterical to say the least for the hierarchy to pay seventy pieces of silver to someone for what was after all a formal identification. There was no danger of Jesus denying who he was or claiming that they had arrested the wrong man. Far too many people knew Jesus, especially among the Pharisees, for there to be any doubt as to his identity even without a formal identification.

The fact that the Sanhedrin panicked and engaged in one of the most unsavoury acts of human history is indicative of the lengths to which they were prepared to go to destroy not only Jesus but his, at the time, puny religion. The words 'Judas' and 'blood money' have passed into the languages of almost every civilised nation as ignominious and hateful qualities.

Why were the Sanhedrin in such a hurry to arrest Jesus? The heavy handed response of the Sanhedrin in sending Judas to betray a preacher who had said very little which was unusual requires some explanation.

JESUS WAS NO GREAT CROWD COMPELLING PREACHER

Despite what modern preachers would have us believe Jesus was NOT a great orator nor was he a great crowd compellor. His message was not at all politically exciting and his pronouncements no more subversive than exhorting them to love one another.

Jesus had not even started another religion, he and his followers were still faithful worshippers in the temple and they observed all the ritual and obeyed all the laws of their faith.

The evidence is that the Sanhedrin wanted Jesus to die and that they had to go to great lengths to persuade him to say the things which they were later to use against him. He had stolidly refused to lead the revolutionaries who undoubtedly saw him as a nationalistic leader and he threatened no one in authority, either Jewish or Roman, except to insist upon a spiritual rather than a formalistic approach to the faith of his fathers.

True he had made a scourge of cords and whipped the traders out of the temple but that would have been more a gesture than an attempt to cause actual pain. Turning the tables over might have warranted some chastisement but certainly NOT crucifixion. Such demonstrations were not unusual in a religion which, despite a certain long-term cohesion, was known for being schismatic in the short term. Judaism was not unused to sects within it's ranks and usually coped with them rather well.

Jesus had likened the Pharisees to a 'generation of vipers' but we must get even that in the context of where and when it was said. He had the right to say it under the law and there could be legally no punishment for that. Far worse things had been said of them before Jesus had arrived on the scene and far worse things were said of them after Jesus had gone but they didn't crucify the people who said them.

There were no microphones, recorders or television cameras present and the Pharisees would know that the words, spoken to a small group of people at what would be the equivalent of an informal meeting on a street corner in England today would not be spread far and wide and would soon be forgotten by those who heard them.

From the point of view of the Romans, though Jesus claimed to be the King of the Jews, it was obvious that he had no intention of plotting the overthrow of Roman rule by force nor taking the throne physically. Arguably Jesus was something of a diversion for the Jewish population, as far as the Romans were concerned, from the more dangerous and violent propagators of Jewish freedom.

THE WANING INFLUENCE OF JESUS

Apart from one or two instances, there is nothing to indicate that, despite his wealthy and influential friends, Jesus wielded great influence. In fact it could be argued with some justification that prior to his crucifixion he had lost most of his followers other than his family and friends.

True a great crowd had gathered and strewn palm leaves in his path and shouted 'Hosannah' but it would seem to have been more of an emotional outburst than any deep seated conviction that the Messiah had indeed come, for, within a short time we see him weeping over Jerusalem because the people of that city had rejected him.

As the prophet had foretold 'He was DESPISED and REJECTED of men and they hid as it were their faces from him'. There WAS the occasional multitude but there is every indication that it was comprised more of the curious than the convinced.

Even the sick he had healed did not come back to give thanks in large numbers, Jesus himself tells us that of ten lepers he healed only one came back to give thanks (Luke 17:17) indicating that despite his miracles Jesus did not have the crowd-compelling magnetism that many before and since him have had. Indeed it would seem that Hitler in the death bunker in Berlin was able to engender much more personal loyalty at the time of his death than Jesus. At least Joseph Goebells was prepared to die with him, Goebells wife was prepared to die with him and they were willing to sacrifice their children on the altar of their adoration. Eva Braun too was prepared to make the supreme sacrifice.

Most of the crowd that cried 'Crucify him, crucify him' must have known of Jesus' works and perhaps many had had relatives healed or had been healed themselves.

Even the disciples slept while Jesus sweated, as it were 'great drops of blood' in Gethsemany. He had engendered so little loyalty in his followers that a foreigner had to help him to carry his cross and Peter denied him for no better reason than that he was being tormented by a serving wench.

There was no loyal tribute to Jesus and no violent demonstration against the execution of Jesus at the foot of the cross, only the women quietly weeping, and if it be argued that the thought of punishment deterred the followers of Jesus from supporting him when he faced crucifixion then I must say that that, in fact, makes my case. Look through history, yes, look around the world today and see how many people are prepared to die horrendous deaths for the people to whom they are devoted.

Jesus spent a lot of his time making the point that he had NOT got a great following, had little influence and had been, in his word, 'rejected'. He was fond of saying 'where two or three are gathered together in my name, there am I in the midst of them' and 'Straight is the gate and narrow the way that leads to life eternal, and few there are that find it.' Jesus did not claim to be a 'crowd compeller'.

Why then should the Jews fear him so much, why should he have engendered such hatred?

THE 'PANIC' TRIAL OF JESUS

There is something which remains unexplained about the speed with which the Sanhedrin held the trial of Jesus. Both his arrest and his trial show every sign of panic on the part of the Sanhedrin.

Let us follow the events leading up to the crucifixion.

It was at night by the light of flaming torches that they went out to arrest Jesus. Jesus walked forward towards the guards and asked them if it was he they had come to arrest.

Judas delivered his kiss of identification. Then something about which we may wonder took place, the priest's guard acting upon the authority of the Sanhedrin made the arrest. It is important to note that Jesus was NOT arrested by the Roman guard as is so often assumed.

Why is that important? Because it was ILLEGAL for the priest's guards to arrest a citizen. The power to arrest a citizen resided solely with the Roman court which ruled Judea and could only be exercised by Roman soldiers by order of the court.

Why should the priesthood, which, it would seem had behaved as legalistically fastidiously, and at great expense, in respect of having Jesus correctly identified by a civilian witness suddenly decide to act illegally and risk Roman retribution in wrongfully arresting Jesus? Even the charge of blasphemy could have waited until after the Passover and have been dealt with in the correct manner. If Jesus had been uttering his 'blasphemy' for over a year then what was the pressing need to stop him within a few hours?

There was, we have to suspect, a much deeper reason for Jesus' execution than the trumped-up charge of blasphemy!

We read of no protest by the Romans! Even the strong defenders of Jesus during his trial, Joseph of Arimathea and other sympathetic members of the of the Sanhedrin, seem not to have queried the legality of Jesus' arrest.

Surely the legality of the arrest of the accused would be used by any defence worth it's salt! It is something, if indeed Jesus was a citizen of Palestine, which would not have escaped the astute mind of Joseph.

The answer may lie in the fact that Jesus had not lived in Palestine for the requisite amount of time to be considered a citizen. Where had he lived?

Even if Joseph of Arimathea had not complained of the illegality of the

Jesus' arrest the Romans would certainly have had something to say to the Sanhedrin. The Romans took a dim view of having their laws overridden but we read of no protest by the Romans! Pontius Pilate would have enjoyed little better than to have brought the Sanhedrin to heel on a point of law.

Having recognised that the Sanhedrin was intent on putting Jesus to death, why did not the defence, even if only as a last resort, call upon the ROMANS to declare the trial illegal?

Why did no one query the validity of Jesus' arrest?

The answer can only lie in the fact that Jesus had not lived in Palestine for the requisite amount of time to be considered a citizen.

We ask again: If Jesus had NOT lived in Palestine long enough to be considered a citizen then where had he lived?

TRIAL AT NIGHT

Jesus was tried during the night!

We are told by Blackstone in his COMMENTARIES ON THE LAWS OF ENGLAND that the Romans did not allow trials after dark especially when it was a trial for the prisoner's life. Yet the legislative members of the Sanhedrin went into emergency session at midnight to try Jesus.

The Sanhedrin had no power to try Jesus on a life or death charge. Trial for life was something which Rome reserved unto itself.

Yet the furious trial went ahead and Caiaphas, the High Priest of Judaism, flew in the face of the might of Rome. Later in the trial, when the defence of Jesus seemed to be winning the day Caiaphas engaged in a travesty of justice which perhaps had not been witnessed in the legal history of the Jews and which has perhaps not been witnessed since. He took the prosecution case out of the hands of the prosecuting council, undertook the prosecution himself. He cross-examined Jesus himself and did not allow the defence the right of reply.

There is no historic record to suggest that Caiaphas was anything other than a sincere follower of his faith and a believer in the sanctity of the law. He seems not to have behaved illegally on other occasions, why did he do so in the case of Jesus? They accused Jesus of blasphemy, and of course they were right to do so if Jesus was not what he claimed to be, but even that does not explain the malpractice of justice and haste with which they despatched Jesus to his death. Had the trial followed the normal pattern, had it taken several weeks or even months, this man who had convinced so few thus far was unlikely to convince many more from prison. The fear, malevolence and haste hid something far more than detestation of a local preacher who proclaimed himself to be God.

The Sanhedrin voted forty to thirty-one for the dismissal of the case against Jesus which would indicate that despsite the manipulations of Caiaphus, despite the intolerable pressures put upon the members of the Sanhedrin to find Jesus guilty and despite the fact Jesus had insulted and maligned many of the members, the majority were convinced of Jesus' innocence.

Ultimately Caiaphus went to the extremity of sending Jesus to be tried before Pontius Pilate on a charge of treason against Rome. It was a charge which Pontius Pilate was to reject with the words 'I find no fault in this man' and with the famous symbolic act of washing his hands. PILATE PRONOUNCED JESUS INNOCENT ON NO LESS THAN FOUR OCCASIONS!

Caiaphus took great personal risks to send Jesus to his death. It has been suggested that he did it to ingratiate himself with Rome but that seems not to be the case. Even after Pilate had said he found no fault in Jesus, a refuge in which Caiaphus could have hidden had he wished, Caiaphus pursued his determination to destroy Jesus and all he stood for. The charge of blasphemy was thrown out by the Sanhedrin and Caiaphus could have accepted that decision honourably but he didn't, why?

Pilate said he found no fault in Jesus, it was a verdict which would have lifted the responsibility from the Jews for any future insurrection which Jesus might have led, if that WAS their fear.

PILATE'S ASTONISHING PASSWORD

One saying of Pilate when Jesus stood before him at the trial may give us a clue. To some it is a philosophical saying but to most it is difficult to understand and seems ill at ease in the context. It is even perhaps, a ridiculous aside for a judge to make during a hearing upon which a man's life depended. Pilate said "What is truth?"

Those three words were passwords used by the British Druids at the beginning of their debates!

There are authorities who contend that Pontius Pilate finished his education IN A DRUID COLLEGE IN ENGLAND.

It is probable that Jesus, Joseph of Arimathea and the affluent and influential followers of Jesus were considered by Caiaphus to be at the centre of something far more deadly to him and the Jews than mere revisionism. Something which would, if not destroyed shake the very foundation of the nation's belief in it's own uniqueness, something in the nature of AN INTERNATIONAL PLOT.

Whether that is so or not is not the essence of this chapter. What I have tried to show here is the extraordinary lengths to which the Jewish authorities went to persecute a preacher who, by his own admission, was not being very successful.

Had Jesus stood at the head of a vast following which threatened either church or state the haste to kill him would have been understandable. He threatened neither church nor state, and, by the time he was arrested it would seem that his popularity was already on the wain.

Caiaphus and his followers must have recognised in Jesus a man of influence and it is obvious from the Bible narrative that that influence was not in Palestine. The whole question of Jesus' influence would seem to indicate that it was outside Palestine — but WHERE?

There was some deadly reason why a Jew, towards whom Pilate seemed almost mysteriously friendly, should so upset Caiaphus. It was a reason seemingly unknown to the majority of the members of the Sanhedrin who voted overwhelmingly in favour of Jesus' release. It was a reason too, destined to bring the most dire persecution on the Jesus family after his ascension and cause Joseph of Arimathea, a band of the followers of Jesus and, we speculate, the Virgin Mary to flee to England.

7 Joseph of Arimathea And The Search For The Holy Grail

There is but a passing reference to Joseph of Arimathea in the Gospels and yet a considerable amount is known about him from secular history and tradition.

Joseph is important to our hypothesis because he is the link between Palestine, the Holy Family and Britain. His kinship to Mary is important because proof of that makes it probable that she and the boy Jesus would be in his guardianship and it is a reasoned presumption that she would go with him on his travels.

The facts about his prominence in business are important and the kind of business he was in is important because that tells us something about where it is likely he would be when he was not in Palestine.

Records of his travels in Western Europe, especially Britain, abound and his influence would seem to have been international.

The breadth of Joseph's influence is difficult to exaggerate. He was a man of great political and religious influence and was eminent in the business world.

Joseph's life is nothing if not incredible. Not only was he an uncle of the Virgin Mary, an uncle of her husband Joseph and great uncle of Jesus but also a respected and influential member of the Jewish Sanhedrin. He has well been called the Onassis of his day by reason of his riches and was a metal dealer and owner of vast tin and lead mine interests in Britain, builder of the first above ground church in the world, 'Nobilis Decurio' or Minister of Mines to the Roman Government and sire of a Queen of the ancient British Royal Family.

His importance in Jesus' band of faithful disciples can hardly be exaggerated and yet he is not mentioned in the New Testament except for that one instance when he went to Pilate and asked for the body of Jesus so that he could bury it in his own tomb.

In the Latin Vulgate of the Gospels of St. Luke and St. Mark Joseph of Arimathea is referred to as 'Decurio' this was a Roman term to denote one who is in charge of mines. St. Jerome in his translation gives Joseph's official title as being 'Nobilis Decurio' a title by which the Roman Minister of Mines was known.

THE FINDING OF JOSEPH'S GRAVE IN BRITAIN

A John Leland, who held Henry VIII's licence to search for ancient records in the abbeys of Britain tells how he examined (in 1534) Maelgwyn of Avalon's Historia de Rebus Britannicis in the Glastonbury Abbey Library and found the following

> 'The Isle of Avalon . . . received thousands of sleepers, among them Joseph de Marmore from Aramathea by name, entered his perpetual sleep. And he lies in a bifurcated line next the southern angle of the oratory made of circular wattles by 13 inhabitants of the place over the powerful adorable Virgin'.

The account goes on to record how when Joseph arrived at Glastonbury he had with him two 'white and silver cruets' which contained the blood and sweat of Jesus.

DID THE VIRGIN MARY STAY WITH FRIENDS OF JOSEPH OF ARIMATHEA IN EGYPT?

It is interesting that Joseph is spoken of as Joseph de Marmore and it has been said that Joseph actually lived in Marmorica in Egypt before he dwelt at, and became known by the name of Arimathea.

If that is so then it would explain the ease with which the Holy Family were able to take up residence in Egypt during the slaughter of the innocents by Herod when Jesus was a child. Without the patronage of someone of wealth, without contacts with whom the family could find accommodation, such a migration would have been perilous if not impossible.

Experienced Egyptologists have from time to time commented on certain Egyptian characteristics of the Chalice Well at Glastonbury, which well is said to have been constructed by or under the supervision of, Joseph. It is of course understandable that the well should have certain Egyptian characteristics if Joseph had had access to Egyptian learning and had other connections there.

JOSEPH'S UNUSUAL REQUEST TO PONTIUS PILATE

Let us look more closely at the incident after the death of Jesus when Joseph went to Pilate and sought the body of Jesus. It is an action which would seem to confirm Jospeh's blood relationship with Jesus.

Remembering the antipathy of the Jewish hierarchy, especially

Caiaphus, at the trial of Jesus there can be no doubt that they would not have wished to have accorded the body of Jesus the dignity of being buried in a rich man's tomb, set in a beautiful garden, if they could have avoided that happening. They would not have permitted Pontius Pilate to behave irregularly in the matter of the disposal of the body of Jesus.

The Sanhedrin would undoubtedly have wished the body of Jesus to be disposed of with the same ignominy as the method of his death. Why should they have any desire to allow Jesus to be buried in a rich man's tomb when the whole idea of the crucifixion had been to destroy Jesus in the most humiliating way possible and bring the standing of Jesus of Nazareth down to that of a common criminal?

There were too, all the attendant problems of having him in a tomb, the accessibility of the tomb to his disciples, the need to guard the tomb for perhaps years after his entombment for Jesus had made an appointment with his disciples THE OTHER SIDE OF DEATH and they knew how disastrous it would be for them if he were able to appear to keep that appointment. Jesus had said he would rise on the third day, to have him thrown into the communal grave with the other crucified malefactors would have ensured that he neither kept his promise, nor appeared to keep his promise.

WHY DID THE SANHEDRIN ALLOW JESUS A MARTYR'S TOMB

Resurrection apart, the Sanhedrin were no less aware of the fact that the dead Jesus could become a martyr than the Allies were aware that Goering, Göebells and the Nazi hierarchy could become martyrs after their death. The bodies of those monsters were, quite rightly, disposed of so that no one could create an aura of martyrdom around their graves and use them as objects of veneration.

Undoubtedly Caiaphas recognised the danger and desired that the body of Jesus be cast into the common pit reserved for common criminals, the pit in which all trace of the identity of the dead person was lost and all trace of his existence obliterated.

There was only one circumstance in which that fate could be avoided under Jewish and Roman law and that was IF A RELATIVE OF THE DEAD PERSON CLAIMED THE BODY.

The very fact that Joseph of Arimathea was able to claim the body of Jesus and inter it in his own tomb is proof enough that he was the closest living male relative of Jesus. It is all but conclusive proof that Joseph was the great uncle of Jesus and supports the evidence that Joseph of Arimathea was uncle both to the Virgin Mary and her husband which is to be found in

Harl. MS in the British Museum and the Jesus College MS. It is a fact also attested to in the Jewish Talmud.

No one but the closest of relatives would have been allowed to have the body of ANY executed criminal. In the case of Jesus, especially in view of the fact that he had proclaimed his own resurrection, it is most certain that only the greatest influence brought to bear on the two vindictive priests Annas and Caiaphas could have allowed Joseph to procure the body of Jesus.

JOSEPH OF ARIMATHEA — FRIEND OF THE ROMANS

The rule of the Sanhedrin was that the body of an executed criminal must be claimed by a relative and buried before sunset. But Joseph did NOT go to the Sanhedrin, he went to Pilate which is yet another indication that though Jesus was a Jew he was NOT a citizen of Palestine. It would add weight to the view that Jesus had lived abroad for the greater part of his life.

Despite the dangers of having Jesus interred in a prestigious tomb with all the attendant difficulties, despite the fact that the Sanhedrin had managed to engineer a criminal's death, despite the fact that the Sanhedrin guards would have to keep a watch on the tomb, perhaps for years, and despite the fact that the body of the man they feared so deeply would be lying within a few minutes walk of the city walls in a beautiful garden tomb, Joseph was successful in his demand for the body.

It would seem that the Roman authorities were far more solicitous of Jesus than most people imagine. As we have seen, they did NOT arrest him. And, we should remember, Pilate DID write the inscription JESUS OF NAZARETH THE KING OF THE JEWS and refused to amend it to JESUS OF NAZARETH WHO SAID HE WAS THE KING OF THE JEWS at the request of the priests. Pilate DID instantly agree to the prestigious burial of Jesus.

The way in which Pontius Pilate behaved throughout the whole affair would seem to indicate Jesus had substantial connections outside Palestine and unconnected with the Jews. It would appear certain that Joseph of Arimathea had considerable influence with the Roman authorities.

If he was their Minister for Mines he WOULD be a very important person for they had failed to subjugate Britain, from whence most of the tin and lead to keep their war machine running came. It was to be many years before the Romans gained enough military ascendancy to take the metals they wanted from Britain without consent.

THE PLOT TO KILL TIBERIUS CAESAR

Pontius Pilate was quite unlike the character people have portrayed him to be. He was in fact a man of considerable bravery but who found himself in unenviable circumstances when it came to the conflict between Jesus and Joseph of Arimathea on the one hand and the priests Annas and Caiaphas on the other.

Carlo Franzen in his MEMOIRS OF PONTIUS PILATE indicates that Caiaphas had information that Pontius Pilate had involved himself in an abortive plot to assassinate Tiberius Caesar. One wonders what knowledge Joseph of Arimathea had of the plot to assassinate one of history's worst perverts and monsters. To what extent was he involved? There would be little doubt that, when he was home from his trips abroad, Joseph, as Minister of Mines would meet and dine with Pilate and other Roman dignitaries.

A careful study of the Gospels shows the surprising fact that Jesus never uttered one word of condemnation of the Romans during his ministry. He seems to have had an empathy with them that went far beyond anything one would expect from a Jew living in an occupied territory. He accepted their taxes with good humour and though he railed against the religious dignitaries of his own faith and criticised his own countrymen for their unbelief he never subjected the Romans to even one of the frequent tongue lashings he seemed to reserve for the religious people of his own race. Even after the Roman soldiers had driven the nails into the hands and feet Jesus prayed 'Father forgive them for they know not what they do'.

Things would not have been made the easier for Pilate when Claudia his wife warned him to have nothing to do with the condemnation of Jesus for Claudia was Tiberius Caesar's step-daughter. Despite the 'sword of Damocles' hanging over his head Pontius Pilate pronounced Jesus guiltless on no less than four occasions.

Through the mists of time we begin to see Joseph of Arimathea as being a man of influence who was politically very much at the centre of the world stage. We shall see later how the disciples of Jesus, far from being the desert wanderers they are so often portrayed, continued at the centre of world affairs befriending the rich and famous and influencing the affairs of men politically as well as spiritually.

THE TIN ISLANDS

The fame, in ancient times, of Britain as the 'Tin Islands' is too well known to be laboured here but, since tin was the business of Joseph of Arimathea it is worthy of mention in passing.

As early as 450 B.C. Herodotus writes of the British Isles as being the 'Cassiterides' or 'Tin Islands'. Sir Edward Creasy in his History of England tells us that 'The British mines mainly supplied the glorious adornment of Solomon's Temple'.

In his short treatise 'Did Our Lord Visit Britain' Rev. Cyril C. Dobson writes 'Pytheaus (352-323 B.C.) mentions the tin trade, as does Polybius (circa 160). Diodorus Siculus gives a detailed description of the trade. He tells us that tin was mined, beaten into squares, and carried to an island called Ictis, joined to the mainland at low tide, which is generally held to be Mount St. Michael in Cornwall'.

The prophet Ezekiel writing about 595 B.C. tells us 'Tarshish was thy merchant by reason of the multitudes of all kind of riches; with silver, iron, tin and lead, they traded in thy (Israel) fairs' Chapter 27:12.

Thus we see from the evidence of the Old Testament that there was a trade in silver, iron, tin and lead prior to the year 600 B.C.

From whence did these commodities come? Encyclopaedia Brittanica throws light on the subject:

> 'It is possible that they (the Phoenicians) reached the coasts of Britain, then called the Cassiterides, or Tin Islands, in search of the tin of Cornwall;'
>
> Page 889. 1973 edit.

It should be remembered that from the earliest days of Israel's seagoing history the ships of Israel sailed with the ships of Phoenicia and they were all called 'Phoenician'.

The Sunday Times Historic Atlas of the World shows that lead and tin mines existed in Britain.

An archaeological dig at Ostia the seaport of Rome, produced an ancient Roman drain-pipe which was bonded with tin. Professor Forbes sent a section to England for analysis and it was found that the metal came from the Mendip Hills which are of course near Glastonbury.

There is lead in the British Museum dated A.D. 60, which bears the inscription 'British lead, the property of the Emperor Nero.'

We begin to see a pattern emerging! The proposition that the Holy Family visited Britain begins to seem less rediculous. Corroberative evidence for Joseph of Arimathea's ties with Britain now flows in from many different and unconnected sources, flowing into the same stream and rushing as a mighty river to the one conclusion.

Is it not reasonable to think that the Minister of Mines of the Roman Empire at war would visit the tin and lead mines upon which the Romans depended so heavily? Is it not reasonable to think that this rich metal merchant with much of his business interests tied up in Britain would come here to ensure their safe and profitable working?

When Joseph, husband of Mary, died, realising that the events surrounding the birth of Jesus would not have been forgotten in his own land and with the persecution by Herod of but twelve years before fresh in their minds, is it not reasonable to think that their rich relative and protector (for such his obtaining of the body of Jesus from Pilate shows him to be) would take them with him wherever he travelled?

Does it not all tie in with the apparent absence of Jesus from the land of his birth?

At the Jubilee celebrations of the late King George V, his Majesty commanded that Blake's Jerusalem be sung. One must wonder in view of the evidence we have read, and will read in later chapters, if the immortal words of the mystical William Blake were rather more than wishful thinking:

And did those feet in ancient time
Walk upon England's mountains green?
And was the Holy Lamb of God
On England's pleasant pastures seen?
And did the Countenance Divine
Shine forth upon our clouded hills?
And was Jerusalem builded here
Among those dark Satanic mills?

8 The First Coming Of Jesus To Britain

There are two mysterious silences in the gospels about the movements, activities and sayings of both the Virgin Mary and Jesus.

We have mentioned the second silence which spans a period of about eighteen years, during which time there is no mention whatever of the activities of either the Virgin Mary or Jesus. That second period of silence commenced after Jesus is recorded as having been at the Passover when he was twelve years of age and ended when he commenced his ministry at the age of thirty-nine years of age.

There is however another 'silence', the first silence, which is meaningful. The silence spans the period between the time the Holy Family came out of Egypt and the incident at the Passover when Jesus was twelve years of age. There is a period of some ten years of the childhood of Jesus about which nothing is written in the gospels and there would appear to be no Palestinian legend or tradition.

Thus, apart from the incident in the synagogue, there is a period of 37 or 38 years during which there is no mention of anything Mary or Jesus said or did.

It is necessary for me again to draw the attention of the reader to the circumstances of the birth of Jesus. It was claimed, at his birth, that this child was God incarnate, the product of a virgin birth. Wise men from the East brought gifts of gold, frankincense and myrrh. Herod conducted the slaughter of the innocent in a bid to destroy the child. Herald Angels proclaimed the coming of the Messiah in the shepherd's fields to the shepherds.

Can we believe that no action nor any utterance of either the Virgin Mary, Jesus or his foster father Joseph was important enough to record? The idea is beyond belief!

Nevertheless, one incident and one incident only, is recorded about the Holy Family's life in 38 years. Only a little over ONE YEAR of Jesus' adult life is recorded.

The solitary incident which IS recorded is a fairly trivial one and there must have been many more important incidents in the life of Jesus. It was not a profound incident, it adds little to what we know about Jesus and it carries no particular gospel message. One is left with the strong feeling that the writer has related the ONLY incident he knew about the childhood of Jesus.

Examining the first silence, we must observe that Jesus must have done and said many things of importance between the time of his birth and his twelfth birthday — why are none of them recorded? Mary must have said and done many things which were more important than those mentioned in the Passover incident — why are THEY not recorded?

It may be argued that the disciples did not know Jesus until he was a grown man but that is not true. As we have seen, almost all his disciples were either family or friends of the family and they would have been quite conversant with what both Jesus and Mary did if they were living in Palestine. Anyway, a child so miraculously born could not have been other than the centre of attention and undoubtedly from a very early age people, especially the sick, would seek his blessing. There is no record of any such thing happening and we are forced to seek a reason for such a surprising state of affairs.

There seems to be no logical reason why there should have been a silence about him from the time he came out of Egypt until he was twelve, then the record of one fairly petty incident, followed by yet another silence regarding his whereabouts and doings.

It does not suffice to say, as some theologians say, that Jesus did not declare himself as Messiah until he was thirty or so years of age. Who Jesus was was declared at his birth in quite unmistakable terms — it was no secret.

If the incident at the Passover at the age of twelve was important enough to warrant mention then there must have been many as important incidents during his early life. We ask again — why are they not mentioned?

The only possible answer is that his disciple relatives DID NOT KNOW ANYTHING ABOUT HIS EARLY LIFE, nor did they know anything about Mary's life when Jesus was young and THAT presupposes that neither he nor Mary were in Palestine.

It is unfortunate for the development of Christian thought that generations of preachers have seen fit to regard the Bible as a 'text mine' rather than a living narrative. The incident in which Jesus became 'lost' for three days when he was twelve years of age has been largely overlooked except for the occasional, inevitable and unimaginative sermon spiritualising the story.

WERE MARY AND JOSEPH NEGLECTFUL PARENTS?

The facts bear some consideration. Mary, Joseph and Jesus had gone to the Passover in Jerusalem and after the Passover celebrations had finished, Mary and Joseph set off for home. We are told that they had travelled 'a day's journey' when they noticed that Jesus was not with them. They then returned to Jerusalem, searched for three days in Jerusalem for him before they finally found him debating with the teachers in the temple.

I would like my readers to put themselves in the position of Mary and Joseph, parents travelling in a land where robbery and murder were not unknown, and ask themselves whether THEY would travel for a whole day assuming that their child was somewhere in the party of relatives and friends. Are we to think of Mary and Joseph as careless parents or is there another explanation?

We are told that even at twelve years of age Jesus was intelligent enough to debate with the teachers in the temple and they were astounded at his ability. Is it not strange then that a boy of such intelligence would allow his parents to leave Jerusalem without letting them know that he was staying behind?

When they found him the first words of Jesus were 'Why are you looking for me?' Would that not indicate that he thought they KNEW he was not going with them? We must wonder at the confidence he displayed in staying in Jerusalem and the surprise he expressed at his parents being worried about him. It is as if he had been away from them for considerable lengths of time before and being away from them was not at all unusual.

WHAT WAS JESUS' RELATIONSHIP TO HIS FOSTER-FATHER JOSEPH

One has to wonder about Jesus' relationship with his foster father Joseph for Jesus gives scant deference to him in this story and Joseph is never mentioned again. 'Don't you know that I must be about my father's business' Jesus says to Mary. He could equally have made the remark less of an affront to Joseph by saying 'Don't you know that I must be about my **heavenly** father's business?'

It is evident that Joseph died when Jesus was very young, probably soon after the Passover incident. Surely, if Jesus had attended the funeral and the Holy Family had been as close knit as is assumed, would not the premature death of Joseph have been a time when Jesus, or Mary, or both would have had something quotable to say or have done something reportable? If Jesus had been at Joseph's bedside when he died and at his tomb when he was buried, would that not have been an incident at least as important as Jesus getting lost for three days in Jerusalem?

No, apart from the scant reference to him, and then not by name, in the Passover story, Joseph is not mentioned in any record after the Holy Family had returned from Egypt when Jesus was a baby.

Even at the time of Jesus' birth, and later in Egypt, there is no record of Joseph doing anything other than obeying the instructions of the angels to the letter, he would hardly have dared do less! But Joseph is not reported to have said one word in support or glorification of Jesus as Messiah. Compare his silence with the magnificat of Mary, the song of Simeon, the enthusiasm of Anna and the poem of praise which Zacharias spoke of his son John.

We are told that when Mary and Joseph found Jesus in the temple Mary said 'Why have you treated us in this way? Your father and I have been searching for you with aching hearts'. Among the Jews the man was head of the house but again it is Mary who speaks, there is no record that Joseph said anything!

The narrative goes on to tell us that Jesus went back with his parents to Nazareth 'but Mary pondered these things in her heart.' Again no mention of Joseph, did HE not ponder these things in HIS heart!

Is all this important? Very! It seems probable that from very early childhood Jesus was in the guardianship of Joseph of Arimathea. Perhaps, though he obeyed the Divine instructions to the letter and was a just man, Joseph, Jesus' foster father, never quite came to terms with the virgin birth. Or it may be that he was persuaded in his own mind that his foster fathership should remain in low profile because of Jesus' Divine nature. On the other hand it may be that he was ailing for a considerable time before his premature death and was glad to have his son in the safe and more affluent care of Joseph of Arimathea.

Whatever the reason the fact remains that Joseph, husband of the Virgin Mary, figures not at all in anything Jesus said or did. That is something that cannot be understood if Jesus spent the first thirty years of his life under Joseph's roof, or even, considering Joseph's early death, the first twelve or thirteen years as Joseph's foster child.

WHO LOOKED AFTER JESUS WHEN HE WAS 'LOST' IN JERUSALEM

It is all part of our regarding Jesus more as a myth than a real person that we do not ask questions about the Bible stories about him. We seem to assume that, even as a lad, he could somehow survive in Jerusalem without anyone looking after him.

Let us look at Jesus' three days without his parents in Jerusalem. Who fed him? Where did he sleep? Who looked after him? He debated with the teachers in the temple. A dirty little boy would not have been allowed to debate with the teachers in the temple and he would most certainly have been dirty, and not a little smelly, in the heat of Jerusalem if he had not bathed and had not had a change of clothing. Why was he allowed to debate in the temple?

The probable answer is that he went there with Joseph of Arimathea, a member of the Sanhedrin and an influence in the temple and John the Baptist's father Zacharias who was a priest at the temple.

It would appear that the only plausible explanation of Jesus' staying behind in Jerusalem was that there was a mistake of intent. He thought his parents realised he was to stay, something he had done before, but THEY did not realise that he was going to do so on this occassion. Had they not been used to Jesus not being with them THEY would have taken greater care to ensure he was in the party at the commencement of the journey and HE would undoubtedly have shown them the courtesy of saying he intended to stay.

JESUS, THE VIRGIN MARY AND THE TRADITIONS OF GLASTONBURY

Not only is there no record of Jesus and Mary being in Palestine during the missing years but there is no tradition of them being there either.

Compare that with the documentation and tradition that exists regarding Jesus and Mary in Britain and one has to ask why it is that no history or tradition exists in the country in which they are KNOWN to have lived and yet at least four separate traditions and a mass of corroborative evidence exist in a country which one would not have expected Jesus to have visited.

Why do these various and largely unrelated traditions interlock, rather as pieces of a jigsaw puzzle?

Corroboration comes from the most surprising quarters. It was not in the interest of either the Roman Catholic Church or St. Augustin to admit that the Roman Church was not the first church in Britain and yet we find St. Augustine (A.D. 597) writing to Pope Gregory:

> 'In the Western confines of Britain there is a certain royal island of large extent, surrounded by water, abounding in all the beauties of nature and necessaries of life. In it the first Neophites of Catholic Law, God hath beforehand acquainted them, found a Church constructed by no human art, BUT BY DIVINE CONSTRUCTION BY THE HANDS OF CHRIST HIMSELF, for the

> salvation of His people. The Almighty has made it manifest by many miracles and mysterious visitations that He continues to watch over it as sacred to Himself, and to Mary, the Mother of God.'

The reference is as quoted by Morgan from 'Epistolae ad Gregoniam Papam'.

Cornish traditions refer to the coming to Britain by the child Jesus accompanied by the Virgin Mary. This would not be a surprising thing to happen after the death of Jesus' foster father, Joseph.

A mother would be loath to be parted from her child for the considerable time it took to make the long and arduous sea journey and undoubtedly Joseph of Arimathea would be loath to leave Mary in the essentially hostile land of Palestine.

If the ancient Breton tradition in Hachette's Guide Bleu, Bretagne is to be accepted the Virgin Mary's links with Western Europe go back even further than any visit she may have made with Jesus when he was a boy. The tradition is that Anna, mother of the Virgin Mary, was born in Cornouaille (Cornwall?) of royal blood. When she was with child she was ill treated by her husband and she fled from Europe to Jaffa from whence she settled in Nazareth where the child was born. The child was Mary who, at the age of fifteen, was married to a carpenter by the name of Joseph.

Though the accuracy of that tradition is not at all vital to our theme, the tradition itself is of interest to us. As with so many traditions, that story seems unbelievable at first but we may reflect upon the fact that Joseph of Arimathea seems to have been accepted quite readily in Britain. From the very commencement, it would seem, he had no difficulty with the language for he was not only able to communicate on normal matters but teach the new religion so convincingly that he was granted twelve hides of land, tax free for himself and his companions. We are led to question why the boy Jesus and his uncle were so readily accepted in a land so far away from their own country.

All that can be readily explained if the mother of the Virgin Mary was of Cornish descent.

Joseph owned tin mines here but how did he come to know about them and how did he come to own them? Why did the disciples fleeing from Palestine during the great persecution come to Britain when there were warmer climes nearer home?

We may reflect too upon the fact that, if the above tradition is true, Anna, Jesus' grandmother would have been a Druid. The Druids had for hundreds of years looked forward to the day when their saviour would come, a saviour by the name of Hesus, the Druidic form of Jesus! Is there not something thought provoking to say the least about the fact that the babe of Bethlehem had the same name as the long expected saviour of the ancient Druids?

THE TRADITIONS OF CORNWALL, SOMERSET AND THE MENDIPS

The traditions of the boyhood visit to Britain are numerous and to be found in Cornwall, Somerset, the Mendip Hills and Glastonbury. It is interesting to note that no such tradition exists in Devonshire and there is little tin mining tradition there.

That fact alone would seem to give substance to the other traditions that Joseph of Arimathea came to Britain because of it's tin production. If the story of Joseph's and Jesus' coming was mere invention why had Devon not originated one? The traditions of Jesus being here invariably exist in the same location as those locations in which there are or have been tin or lead mines. This ties in with the fact that Joseph of Arimathea was a metal merchant and mine owner. It is of interest that when tin was flashed even into this century the workers shouted 'Joseph was in the tin trade'. In Baring Gould's 'Book of Cornwall' he writes:

> 'Another Cornish story is to the effect that Joseph of Arimathea came in a boat to Cornwall, and brought the boy Jesus with him, and the latter taught him how to extract tin and purge it from it's wolfram'.

There are few authorities who would not agree that Joseph, Mary's husband died when Jesus was quite young. We know of no authority who would deny that according to Jewish custom and law, and Roman custom and law, guardianship of a fatherless minor was the responsibility of an uncle.

It is unbelievable that Joseph of Arimathea would abrogate his responsibility for any length of time, certainly not the length of time it would take him to make his sea voyages to Britain and back to Palestine and we can therefore give credence to the various traditions which abound in the West Country of Britain about Jesus' coming as a child to these shores.

The fact that he came here again as a young man and probably stayed for several years is the subject of our next chapter.

9 Jesus In Britain Around 27 A.D.

Some authorities suggest that Jesus made two or more visits to Britain, one as a child and at least one when he was a young man. Be that as it may, it is doubtful that he returned to the Holy Land until he was thirty-nine or so years of age.

We have mentioned the fact that John the Baptist seemed not to know Jesus and that suggests that he had not seen Jesus for a very long time. Had Jesus been in Palestine they would have met at least three times a year at the three great feasts of the Jewish faith to which attendance was mandatory under Mosaic Law.

It is unlikely that Jesus was thirty years of age when he commenced his ministry in Palestine as is so often thought to be the case. It is more probable that he was about forty. This would explain the statement of the Jews as recorded by John when they said to Jesus:

> 'Then said the Jews unto him, Thou art not yet fifty years old, and hast thou seen Abraham?'

It would not be an unusual thing to say of a man passing forty, but a very strange thing to say to a man when he was thirty. It is, apart from the passover incident when he was a child, and a mention by Luke which shows surprising uncertainty, the only time his age was mentioned.

Luke says that at his baptism 'Jesus began to be about thirty years of age' which is in fact only the same as saying of someone 'they are in their thirties.' Of course Luke was writing about 25 years after Jesus' baptism and his remark is made as an introduction to a genealogy in which Jesus' exact age was not of importance.

Ferrar Fenton in his translation of the Bible removes the genealogy and the reference to Jesus' age saying 'I am, therefore perfectly satisfied that it is merely a note of some early editor, and never formed part of St. Lukes Gospel.'

Even if we allow it to stand, Luke's remark does show that he had no documentary evidence of Jesus' age to hand and that there was surprisingly little known about Jesus in his own land. We would not grace it with the name of evidence but this generalisation by one of Jesus' closest disciples is at least suggestive of Jesus' absence from Palestine for a protracted period.

It was not until 29 A.D. that John the Baptist began to preach, as Luke tells us in his Gospel:

> 'Now is the fifteenth year of the reign of Tiberius Caesar, Pontius Pilate being governor of Judea, and Herod being tetrarch of Galilee . . . Annas and Caiaphas being the high priests, the word of God came unto John' 3:1-2.

The fifteenth year of the reign of Tiberius was A.D. 29. Realising that Jesus was born in 7 B.C. he would be thirty six years of age when John BEGAN to preach and it was not until towards the end of John's ministry that Jesus was Baptised.

Authorities differ as to the exact year of Jesus' crucifixion but the generally accepted crucifixion dates are A.D. 31-A.D. 33. The former date would make Jesus thirty eight years of age and the latter would make him forty years of age when he was crucified.

If John had not seen Jesus from the time he was twelve until he suddenly appeared on the banks of the Jordan and considering the fact Jesus would have grown a beard, it is to be expected that the Baptist would not know him.

NUMEROLOGY AND THE NUMBER FORTY

Numerology is very important in the Scriptures, the 33 year period has no significance whatsoever but 40 is a time period which would identify Jesus in Jewish eyes with so many of the great events of their faith:

As Pollock has pointed out in his excellent book THE TABERNACLE'S TYPICAL TEACHING:

> 'Forty is compounded of ten times four. Ten is the measure of man's responsibility Godward and manward, four representing that which is universal. It sets forth the FULL MEASURE OF PROBATION AND TESTING'.

I do not quote Mr. Pollock in any way to infer he would agree with any of my conclusions regarding the age of Jesus.

There are indications throughout the Bible of the symbolism of the number forty.

> The flood was on the earth for FORTY DAYS.
> Noah waited FORTY DAYS after the waters subsided before he opened the Ark.
> Moses was FORTY YEARS old when he fled from Egypt.
> It was FORTY YEARS later that he delivered his people from bondage in Egypt.
> Israel was in the wilderness for FORTY YEARS.
> King Saul reigned for FORTY YEARS.
> King David reigned FORTY YEARS.
> King Solomon reigned FORTY YEARS.
> Nineveh was given FORTY DAYS to repent.
> Jesus was tempted FORTY DAYS in the wilderness.
> There were FORTY DAYS between Jesus' resurrection and his ascension.

That Jesus was about forty years of age when he was crucified brings into focus a quotation from the historian Gildas who wrote A.D. 516-570:

> 'Christ, the True Sun, afforded His Light, the knowledge of His precepts, to this island (Britain) during the height of the reign of Tiberius Caesar'.

The last year of the reign of Tiberius Caesar was A.D. 37. The height of Tiberius' reign was between the years A.D. 20 and 27. On this reckoning Jesus would have been in Britain at that time.

KING INA'S CHARTER

A chapter from a charter given to Glastonbury by King Ina about A.D. 700 is quoted by William of Malmesbury as reading:

> 'To the ancient Church, situated in the place called Glastonbury

> (which Church the Great High Priest and Chiefest Minister formerly THROUGH HIS OWN MINISTRY, and that of angels, sanctified by many an unheard-of miracle to Himself and the ever-virgin Mary as was formerly revealed to St. David) . . .!'

There is only one Great High Priest recognised in the Christian Faith and we find him identified in the Epistles of Paul:

> 'Which hope we have as an anchor of the soul, both sure and steadfast, and which entereth into that within the veil,
> Where the forerunner is for us entered, even Jesus, made an HIGH PRIEST for ever after the order of Melchisedek' Heb. 6:19-20.

Every Christian theologian knew that THE GREAT HIGH PRIEST of the Christian faith was none other than Jesus himself.

We must ask why Jesus would choose to spend so long a time in Britain. It is possible he and Mary would have little choice when Jesus was very young because of the dangers which lurked in the Holy Land. Joseph of Arimathea would not be able to stay at home, not only his business interests would preclude that but his official position with the Roman government would disallow it. There was possibly no choice but for the mother and child to go with him.

It would undoubtedly be a convenient thing for Jesus and Mary to do when Jesus was young because Joseph traded with the British Isles but one would have thought Jesus would have wished to return to his homeland when he had reached his majority. By that time he could have taken care of Mary himself. That Jesus did not return to Palestine is evident from the fact that John the Baptist did not know him and that Jesus paid the 'stranger tax'.

The overwhelming likelihood is that Jesus had been in Palestine a very short time, almost certainly less than a year, when John baptised him otherwise, as I have said, it is certain they would have met at one of the three mandatory annual religious festivals. It is unthinkable that the families would be at the same religious festival and not speak to each other. Judaism is a family centred faith.

Could there have been another reason other than mere expediency that Jesus would have come to Britain and have stayed so long.

THE BRITISH DRUIDS

Where other than Britain could Jesus have gone? Would it have been edifying for him to dwell in Pagan Rome with it's obscenities and cruelties? Could he have felt at home in Greece with it's multiplicity of Gods and perversions?

The whole of Europe, from the Rhine to Spain and from the Euphrates to Calais was tainted with the depraved paganism of Rome. Even the Druidism of Gaul had become bastardised by Roman paganism and had adopted that which was abominated by every Israelite — human sacrifice.

Only in Britain was there a fountain of pure religion flowing, a religion which was uncannily similar in character to the religion of Israel.

R. W. Morgan in his excellent work 'St. Paul in Britain' writes of the British Druids:

> 'Westward of Italy, embracing Hispania, Gallia and the Renish frontiers, portions of Germany and Scandinavia, with it's headquarters and GREAT SEATS OF LEARNING fixed in Britain, extended the Druidic religion. There can be no question that this was the primitive religion of mankind, covering at one period in various forms the whole surface of the ancient world.
>
> The ramifications of Druidism penetrated, indeed, into Italy, Greece, and Asia Minor; nor did Plato hesitate to affirm that all the streams of Greek philosophy were to be traced, not to Egypt, but to the fountains of the West. The pre-historic poets of Greece anterior to the mythological creations of Homer and Hesiod, were, as their names imply, Druids . . .'

Theologically Jesus would have been stifled in the legalistic attitude adopted in the Temple and Synagogues of his day. When he returned to Palestine and commenced his ministry we see how far he had departed from the traditions of his fathers whilst still adhering strictly to the Divine Revelation of the books we now know as the Old Testament.

BRITAIN A CENTRE OF LEARNING IN THE ANCIENT WORLD

There is considerable evidence to support Morgan in his assertion that Britain was, even before the time of Christ, a centre of learning in the world.

Far from being the 'painted savages' of Caesar's war propaganda the British excelled over both the Greeks and the Romans in their culture and learning.

In one of the most profusely and carefully documented books the author has read on the subject Isabel Hill Elder writes:

> 'Concerning the educational facilities available to the so-called barbarous people of these islands, there were at the time of the Roman invasion FORTY DRUIDIC CENTRES OF LEARNING . . . The students of these colleges numbered at times sixty thousand of the youth and young nobility of Britain and Gaul. Caesar comments on the fact that the Gauls sent their youth to Britain to be educated' Celt, Druid and Culdee. Page 54.

That Jesus had had a superb education by the time he returned to Palestine is beyond doubt. That it had not been a typical Jewish education is also beyond doubt.

Even we who believe Jesus to be God manifest in the flesh must accept that when he took upon himself the limitations of an ordinary human being he also took upon himself the need to be educated in the normal way. He could hardly have been 'tempted in all things as we are' if his limitations had not been much the same as ours. We must assume then that his knowledge and debating ability must have been brought about by the same process of learning as is undergone by any other human being.

The way Jesus was able to confound the Pharisees and Sadducees, themselves no mean practitioners of the art of debate, indicates that he had had a considerable education. Even a Roman sent to arrest Jesus came back without having done so and exclaimed 'Never a man spake like this man'.

Nowhere in Europe would Jesus have been more readily accepted than here in Britain. Nowhere else in Europe could he have had the confidence that after his death there would be a safe refuge for his mother Mary and Joseph of Arimathea.

THE ENEMIES OF JESUS WAIT TO POUNCE

When Jesus returned to Palestine it did not take long, a few weeks in fact, for the fury of the established 'church' to descend upon his head, from the first days of his ministry there was an onslaught on him.

Had Jesus continued to live in Palestine as a young man, doubtless, in view of the mysterious happenings which had attended his birth, he would have been constantly the centre of attention and controversy and there would have been questions asked of him and an enquiry by the Sanhedrin.

We are told they accused him of blasphemy because he claimed to be God, that claim was not new, it was made at his birth. Why did they not accuse him of blasphemy sooner?

Had he been in Palestine no doubt the question would have been asked of him during his youth and he would have had to give an honest answer. That it was not asked of him before he was forty or so years of age would seem to be further evidence of Jesus not having lived for long in the land of his birth.

We have seen that the first reason why Jesus and presumably Mary would have come to Britain and stayed here is that of convenience, for it was the place, because of Joseph of Arimathea, to which he had easy transport.

ANCIENT BRITAIN — LAND OF LIBERTY

His second reason for coming here would be that it was at that time the only land in which high educational standards, the rule of equitable law and liberty were assured to all. He would undoubtedly be impressed by the law of Molmutius (450 B.C.) which stated 'There are three tests of civil liberty; equality of rights; equality of taxation; freedom to come and go'.

In Britain there were none of the bestial games which disgraced the so called civilisation of Rome and which, when they were introudced into Athens, caused even the cynics to say, 'We must first pull down the statue to mercy which our forefathers erected fifteen hundred years ago.'

THE RELIGION OF THE DRUIDS

Perhaps more important to Jesus and Mary than the convenience factor, the educational facilities and the political stability existing in Britain at that time would be the fact that the Druid religion was so like the religion of the Hebrews.

Of course there were differences of expression and emphasise, but one might as well argue that a Welsh Chapel and a Greek Orthodox Church have not come from the same faith because they are different in a number of respects, as to argue that Druidism and the Hebrew faith are not kindred because there are differences between them. It is much safer to judge kinship by similarities rather than differences.

The similarities between Druidism and the ancient faith of Israel is startling.

True there were, as we have said, bastardisations of Druidism and careless writers are prone to accept any scrap of evidence found anywhere in the world as being indicative of mainstream Druidism. Are we to accept that because SOME Israelites worshipped a Golden Calf that that was the religion of Israel? Think, if we did not have the Biblical record and had an archaeologist dug the Golden Calf up, what the assumption would have been. Certainly, without other evidence they would have thought that to be typical of the worship of ancient Israel! There WAS a time when Israel worshipped a Golden Calf but we know it was not typical, it was an aberration for which Moses judged them severely.

Yet historians have chosen to generally malign the Druids because they have found 'evidence', but evidence of what they are not sure, evidence perhaps that someone was engaged in a malpractice of their faith? Think of what archaeologists of the future may make of evidence of a Black Mass culled from the remains of such a practice, if they assume it to be the true mass as celebrated by twentieth century Christians. Would they, if they were careless of other evidence, think that that was the way the Christian Church celebrated mass in our day?

WILL OUR MARTYRDOMS LOOK LIKE HUMAN SACRIFICES TO FUTURE GENERATIONS?

What, if the world should survive that long, will men make of the archaeological remains of a martyrdom? Will they assume that Christians in our time practised human sacrifice? Indeed, little can be said of the martyrdoms of Protestants by Catholics or the martyrdom of Catholics by Protestants other than that they WERE sacrifices to placate their God. They each believed it was God's will that they should rid the world of heretics and they each believed that God would be angry with them and punish them if they did not do so. It is one of the horrendous facts of religion that the religious perform their murders so sincerely! But they were MISTAKEN sacrifices.

That such remains may be found two thousand years from now will prove nothing abut Christianity except that at certain times in it's history it has suffered more from it's exponents than from it's opponents and that it has usually had a lot of very mistaken people in it's ranks.

If future generations were to go back to the pure sources of Christianity they would find that such episodes were aberrations on the face of true Christianity not a part of the faith.

THE DRUIDS AND THE DOCTRINE OF VICARIOUS SACRIFICE

When Caesar wrote 'The Druids teach that by no other way than the ransoming of man's life by the life of man, is reconciliation with the divine justice of the immortal gods possible' he was writing the truth.

The Druids DID believe that but when the corrupted Druids of Europe and elsewhere practised human sacrifice it was because of a misconstruction of the meaning of that doctrine.

'The ransoming of man's life by the life of a man' expressed no other truth than the very same truth that had been expressed by the Hebrew prophet Isaiah when he wrote, looking forward to Jesus' day:

> 'He was wounded for our transgressions, he was bruised for our iniquities and by his stripes are we healed'

It expressed no different a truth than that of the Wesleyan hymn:

> 'And can it be that I should gain, an interest in the Saviour's blood?
> Died he for me who caused his pain, for me who him to death pursued.
> Amazing love! How can it be, that thou my God shouldst died for me?'

It is not surprising that, having an eternal God named Hesus (Jesus), the Druids also had the doctrine of vicarious sacrifice. Of course the world would not understand the doctrine of the atonement any more than it does today. There are still those who call Christianity 'a slaughterhouse religion' because they do not grasp the significance of Jesus' death on Calvary.

Stories of Druidic human sacrifices were probably told by the Romans because they did not understand the doctrine of the atonement and they misunderstood the prophecies regarding the man who was born to die and died to deliver. They would need no persuasion to propagate anything they considered to be derogatory to the people they so cruelly treated. The fact is that no evidence of human sacrifice has ever been found in Britain.

THE 'MAGIC' OF THE DRUIDS

Then there are stories of 'magic' being practised among the Druids.

Abaris, who visited Greece, was, according to the Greeks supposed to have possessed the 'Arrow of Apollo', a magical contrivance that Abaris only had to consult to be guided wherever in the world he wished to go.

Abaris DID indeed possess such an 'arrow', and a very small arrow it was. It DID guide him wherever he wanted to go! The Druids had a knowledge of magnetism and the 'Arrow of Apollo' was nothing more than a magnetic needle he used as a compass!

The Druids were accused of sorcery because, it was said, they could bring the moon down to earth. What they actually did was use telescopes which less intelligent peoples equated with 'bringing the moon down to earth' because that is the way it looked to them.

Druid animal sacrifices were no different in kind from the animal sacrifices of the Old Testament. Certainly one cannot level a charge of barbarism at the Druids because of them.

THE DRUIDS AND THE CROSS

One of the most interesting aspects of Druidism is the so called 'sacred tree'. They chose a tree with two principle branches outstretched in the shape of a cross. Central and above the other names they carved the name of their God 'Thau' and beneath the names of his three manifestations Taranis, Belenis and Hesus. The name of Hesus (Jesus) was cut on the right branch and it is worthy of note that when Jesus ascended into heaven it is said he sat 'at the right hand of God the Father'.

Is it but another coincidence that the expected Messiah of Israel was referred to as 'The Branch' or have we to say with Sir Norman Lockyer 'I confess I am amazed at the similarities (to the Old Testament faith) we have come across.' or with William Stukeley 'I plainly discerned that the religion professed by the ancient Britons was the simple patriarchal religion.'

It would seem that the Druids had preserved much of the patriarchal faith that had been corrupted in it's homeland. They believed in the immortality of the soul, and they believed in the resurrection of the body. Despite the clear statement in the Book of Job 'Though my body the worms destroy yet in my flesh shall I see God' few Jews believed in the resurrection of the body. Yet the fact that the belief HAD belonged to their body of truth is seen from that scripture.

Josephus the Jewish historian describing the loaves on the table in the Temple in Jerusalem writes: 'The loaves on the table, twelve in number, symbolized the circle of the Zodiac.' Precisely the same signs, twelve in number were to be found in Druid worship — yet another coincidence?

The Israelites were not allowed to hew stone for their altars for they were instructed 'Thou shalt use no tool upon my altar'. The Druids did not hew stone for THEIR altars. Jacob slept with his head on a stone at Bethel. The Irish Druids had a central stone in THEIR circle which they called — Bethel!

We may well ask how there comes to be such a close similarity between the worship of ancient Israel in the Holy Land and the worship of the Druids in ancient Britain.

ONE GOD BUT MANY MANIFESTATIONS

The Israelites believed that their form of worship was revealed to them by the Great Universal Spirit who they called Jehovah, a being who existed essentially as a spirit. The Druids believed that THEIR religion was a revealed religion, revealed to them by their triune God, who, though worshipped, as was the Israelite's God, through a physical manifestation, was — A SPIRIT.

That Druidism had more than three names for it's godhead is not different from the Israelite's teaching of the nature of God for they from time to time refered to their God as Jehovah, Yahwee, Jekovah Jireh, Jehovah Nissi, Jehovah Shalom all of which were attributes of God rather than different gods. As one person can be a father, a son, a cyclist, a pedestrian, a motorist, a golfer and a gardener so the various names for the one God used by both the Hebrews and the Druids were descriptive of the manifestation, not an indication of a multiplicity of gods.

It would be easy, if the scriptures had not been preserved for us as well as they have, to attribute most of the vices that various writers have attributed to Druidism to the ancient Hebrew faith also.

A display of the supernatural and a display of magic are very similar when witnessed from a position of impartiality. By what authority, for example, do we say of the miracles of the Old Testament that they are of God and of any unusual practice of the Druids that it was magic? We know the supernatural happenings of the Old Testament to be of God because the Scriptures tell us so but that is internal evidence and many of them look mighty like 'magic' to someone who does not believe in the inspiration of the Scriptures.

Caesar, writing in 54 B.C. tells us: 'The Druids make the immortality of the soul the basis of ALL their teaching, holding it to be the principle incentive and reason for a virtuous life.'

THE ORIGINS OF DRUIDISM

We are indebted to R. W. Morgan for his in-depth study of Druidism. I can do no better than quote him at length:

'Druidism was founded by Gwyddon Ganhebon, supposed to be

the Seth of the Mosaic genealogy, in Asia, in the year when the equinox occurred in the first point of Taurus; or the constellation of the Bull. Every year the equinoctial year is completed about twenty minutes before the sun has made a complete revolution from a certain star to the same star again. This arises from the precession of the equinoxes, or from the slow revolution of the pole of the equator round that of the ecliptic. In 25,920 years the pole of the equator makes one entire revolution round that of the ecliptic: hence the equinoctial colure occurs before it did the preceding year. In 72 years the precession amounts to one degree. If therefore, we have the equinoctial or solstitial point given in the ecliptic at any unknown period, it is easy to discover, by comparing it with the present solstitial point, how long that period is past. When the Druid system was founded, the equinox, on the 1st May, occurred in the first point of Taurus, which first point is now, on first of May, 80 degrees from this solstitial point. It requires 72 years to recede one degree. Eighty degrees multiplied by 72 gives 5,760, the exact date when Druidism commenced, i.e., 3903 years before the Christian era . . .

From Asia Druidism was brought into Britain by Hu Gadarn, or the Mighty, its first colonizer, a contemporary of the Patriarch Abraham, under his successors, Plennydd, Goron, Alawn, and Rhivon, it assumed it's complete organisation, becoming both the ecclesiastical and civil constitution of the island.

Morgan quotes Taliesin, the prince-Bard and Druid 'Christ, the Word from the beginning, was from the beginning our teacher, and we never lost his teaching. Christianity was a new thing in Asia, but there never was a time when the Druids of Britain held not it's doctrines.'

When Jesus came to Britain he came to a land where his name was already worshipped, a land which had received it's faith from Seth. He came to a land whose people believed in one God in three manifestations and who accepted the immortality of the soul, the resurrection of the body, the atonement concept, laws which were very similar to the laws that had been delivered to his forefathers in the Old Testament and acknowledged the sign of the cross.

That is why Druidism and Christianity merged without conflict and probably one of the TWO most important reasons why Jesus and Mary would choose this island as their home from home.

The other very important reason why they would come here is examined in another chapter.

10 The Origins Of The English Speaking Peoples

Have you ever wondered from whence the people who first inhabited the British Islands came?

You may ask the question where you will and you will receive conflicting, sometimes uninformed and often very unintelligent answers. It would seem that many historians find it sufficient for their purpose to consider that British history proper began with the coming of the Romans. It is a phenomenon which is perhaps to be expected given the Anglo-Saxon bent for self-denigration.

Yet, despite even that unfortunate national characteristic, it is surprising that there has not been a more thorough investigation into the origins of the English speaking peoples. It IS a subject which is of direct importance to almost half the population of the world, to those many people who have either sprung from our Island stock or have seen their nations transformed by contact with our armies, colonisers and explorers.

The importance of the role played by the English speaking peoples in the history of this planet can be seen in the fact that OUR language has become an international, if not THE international language. It is spoken by more people than any other language either past or present is spoken. The English speaking peoples of the world are held together in a common bond which unites more people than the Chinese or Russian nationalities.

Few will have read this far without realising that there is something very special, though largely unrecognised as yet, about our race and the nations which have sprung from it. In fact, had some dramatic novelist invented the story of how this island came to be inhabited it could not have been more romantic and dramatic than it is in fact.

As we search for the answer to our question 'Did the Virgin Mary live and die in England' the questions crowd in on us.

Why did the Messiah of Israel and his mother spend so much time in these Islands?

Why was the religion of the Druids when he came here so similar to the religion of his homeland?

Why was his name, Jesus, already worshipped here?

What was the magic of the islands?

In his 'Dictionary of Word Origins', published by the Philosophic Library, New York, Joseph T. Shipley writes:

> 'Not two per cent of our English words first rose in the British Isles. Somewhere in the Near East they seem to have started, in that Garden of Eden of earliest man. By one path they wandered up rivers, breasting the Danube into the heart of Europe, roaming westward with the Teutons and the Anglo-Saxon speech.'

If the origins of our language are to be found in the Middle East, if the origins of the Druid faith are to be traced from the Middle East and so many aspects of the teachings of the Druidic faith are seen to be so similar to those of the patriarchal (Hebrew) faith, then could it be that the British nation originated in the Middle East?

JESUS' REMARKABLE STATEMENT

Not long before he died Jesus made a statement which on the face of it seems not to be understandable. He said 'I came not but to the lost sheep of the House of Israel'.

Can we not draw two reasonable conclusions from that statement? The first conclusion being that he spent the 'missing' thirty eight or so years of his life, the years he DID NOT SPEND WITH THE JEWS, residing with the House of Israel? The second conclusion which we may draw is a corollary of the first and that is that the nation in which Jesus spent the majority of his earthly life WERE the 'lost sheep of the House of Israel'.

On another occasion Jesus made an equally remarkable statement to the Jews when he told them that he would take the kingdom from them and give it to a nation 'bringing forth the fruits thereof'.

I must ask my reader not to 'skip' any of the following arguments and, if necessary, to read them as many times as it takes to understand them. Much of our hypothesis that the Virgin Mary lived, died and was buried in England hinges on them. I confess, you may find the next few pages less interesting than I hope you will find the rest of the book. They have to do with a people who existed in ancient times and a place then remote from the British Isles. I hope, when I assure you that what follows is essential to the development of our theme, you will persist in thoroughly reading and understanding every page because the implications of these few less than exciting pages are as thrilling as any detective story.

THE ANCIENT WORLD

We have seen that there are links between Druidism and the patriarchal faith of the Hebrews, and that, among the similarities, not the least important is that both taught the immortality of the soul and the resurrection of the body and both looked forward to the coming of a Messiah. Amazingly, in both cases, the name of that Messiah was to be 'Jesus'.

It would seem natural to assume that the two faiths had a common origin and we must therefore examine the Patriachal faith to see if there is any clue to how the ancient British faith came to be so like the ancient Hebrew faith.

The Patriarchal faith began in the highly civilised Ur of the Chaldees when Abraham, then Abram was called by Jehovah to dwell in another country (Genesis 12).

It is quite astounding how some people seem to find it impossible to be religious without thinking in terms of poverty, sickness, famine, death and 'simplicity'. Their religious heroes have to be both poor and, uneducated to the point of daftness. It is true that Jesus said we should become 'as little children' but he meant we should become childLIKE Not childISH.

Abraham was NOT a poor man and he was NOT an uneducated man.

It says little for the religious critics of ancient scriptures that a century ago they were thinking of Abram and Ur as legends because no trace could be found of Ur of the Chaldees.

Fortunately, as so often happens, science, in this case the science of archaeology, had more faith than the higher critics and work on discovering the site of Ur of the Chaldees continued until Mr. J. E. Taylor, the British Consul at Basra uncovered the evidence for it's existence in 1854. Far from being the simple, nomadic society that had always been associated with Abraham, Ur of the Chaldees was shown to have been a highly sophisticated society and it's citizens were shown to have had a very high standard of education. It was yet another, among hundreds, of instances of doubts about the veracity of the scriptures being resolved when human knowledge had progressed. In 'Documents of Destiny' published by the Covenant Publishing Company. F. Walter Connon writes 'Abram left the city of UR, a city of high civilization and of industry . . .'

GOD'S CHOSEN PEOPLE

Modern thought is very much against anything which smacks of national preference. However we should not ignore the fact that it is claimed by the writers of the scriptures that 'all' scripture was written by instruction 'inspiration' of the Great Universal Spirit.

Now it is obvious that a great universal spirit which was at all times in accord with 'modern thought' would be forever changing it's character because it is one of the lessons of history that the human view of morality and rightness is neither static throughout the generations nor international.

As one scientist so pertinently replied when asked what he thought of the view of modern science on evolution 'I don't know, I haven't read this morning's newspaper!'

It is unfortunate that very early on in human history man decided to create God in his own image. The 'god made in man's image' is, of course, ever changing. From time to time he has been racist and anti-racist, pro-slavery and anti-slavery, Capitalist and Communist, Catholic and Protestant, pro-war and anti-war, pro-abortion and anti-abortion — he has even been anti-Semitic!

God has been made to be whatever the people who believe in him WANT him to be.

We may like what the scriptures teach or we may not like what the scriptures teach but it is doubtful if our likes or dislikes will succeed in changing the nature of the Great Universal Spirit. It is wholly erronious to assume that those parts of the scriptures with which we agree are right and those parts of the scriptures with which we disagree are wrong. With what logic do we assume that the inspiration behind the scriptures must be like us and have OUR morality?

The fact is that, according to the scriptures, the Great Universal Spirit DID choose men and nations FOR NO OTHER REASON THAN THAT IT WAS HIS WILL TO DO SO. He chose ONE nation from ALL the nations on earth and THAT NATION WILL ULTIMATELY RULE THE WORLD!

You don't like the idea? Don't blame the writer I'm only telling you what the Good Book says and don't blame God — He won't take a blind bit of notice of you!

It is probably the 'Achilles Heel' of the Christian church that it markets God in very much the same way as a detergent manufacturer markets soap powder. In a primitive form of market research they ask, 'What do people want, what will they buy? Alright let's make something like that!' So our churches produce a god that is acceptable to their 'buying public' and God becomes packaged according to current fad irrespective of whether that fad is jingoistic or pacific.

As the Baptist preacher the late Charles Haddon Spurgeon a little cynically remarked 'Men will have God anywhere except on his throne'.

THE HISTORY OF THE PATRIARCHAL STATE OF ISRAEL

Whatever our views about national pre-eminence, whether it be right or wrong in our eyes, there can be no doubt that the prophets taught that God DID grant a special place in history to ONE NATION — ISRAEL.

Here's how the ancient nation of Israel came into being.

It is important to know that Abram — later renamed Abraham — was a Shemite, HE WAS NOT A JEW NOR AN ISRAELITE.

Abram dwelt in Ur of the Chaldees and, as we have said, moved out and became father of the Arab, Israelite and many of the Asiatic, people.

Because most people will not look up references I will quote fully the relevant Bible texts. Even if you do not accept the Bible as being inspired it IS the book upon which the national life of the people of Israel was, and to a large extent, still is, based. The Bible is important therefore because it is not until we understand it that we can understand what motivated Israel and, until we can understand that, we cannot understand the history of the patriarchal period.

God is said to have made 'promises' to Abraham, and of course this motivated Abraham and his progeny to behave in a certain way. These promises were passed down from generation to generation and we shall trace the channel through which the 'chosen race' ran.

> 'And God said unto Abraham, As for Sarai thy wife, thou shalt not call her name Sarai, but Sarah shall her name be. And I will bless her, and she shall be a mother of nations; kings of people shall be of her. Then Abraham fell upon his face and laughed, and said in his heart, Shall a child be born to him that is a hundred years old? And shall Sarah that is ninety years old bear? . . .
> And God said, Sarah, Thy Wife, shall bear thee a son indeed; and thou shalt call his name Isaac:- and I WILL ESTABLISH MY COVENANT WITH HIM FOR AN EVERLASTING COVENANT and with his seed after him.'
>
> Genesis 17:15-19

THE SONS OF ISAAC

So Isaac inherited the promise. Isaac was NOT a Jew nor was he an Israelite, he was a Shemite and a Hebrew.

> 'And Isaac was forty years old when he took Rebekah as his wife,

the daughter of Bethuel the Syrian of Padan-aram, the sister to Laban the Syrian.
And Isaac entreated the Lord for his wife because she was barren; and the Lord was entreated by him, and Rebekah, his wife conceived.
And the children struggled together within her; and she said, If it be so, why am I thus? And she went to enquire of the Lord.
And the Lord said unto her, TWO NATIONS ARE IN THY WOMB, and two manner of people shall be born of thee; one shall be stonger than the other people; and the elder shall serve the younger. And when her days to be delivered were fulfilled, behold, there were twins in her womb. And the first came out red, all over like a hairy garment; and they called his name Esau (meaning 'man of the earth')
And after that came his brother out, and his hand took hold on Esau's heel; and his name was called Jacob.

Genesis 25:20-26

Just as Ishmael was the FIRST son of Abraham and should therefore have inherited the promise, so Esau was the FIRST son of Isaac and should have inherited the promise. In both cases we are told that a higher will prevailed. A clear demonstration of the 'God who does according to his own will'.

The boys grew and we are told that Esau became a hunter and Jacob a quiet man 'dwelling in tents'.

Esau came in from the fields one day feeling faint, though, it would seem, his faintness was a very serious nature for he said to his brother Jacob 'I am at the point to die:' Jacob was at the time preparing food and his stricken brother asked him for food.

It always makes historic events more vivid if we relate them to today so think of what follows in today's terms. What would you think of someone who struck this kind of bargain with a brother who was seriously ill?

Jacob said to Esau 'Sell me this day thy birthright . . . swear to me this day; and he (Esau) swore unto him: and he sold his birthday unto Jacob. Then Jacob gave Esau bread and pottage of lentils;' (Genesis 25: parts of 31 and 33). It is obvious that Jacob was not, as our American cousins would say 'A nice guy'!

Yet, it is said, God chose Jacob and heaped blessings upon him. Which just goes to show that the God of Israel did not behave by the rules as WE would conceive the rules but, to utter a colloquialism 'Did things the way he jolly well wanted to do them'.

There is no doubt that we would find Jacob's behaviour disgraceful. Yet

God blessed him and chose him as the founding father of the nation of Israel.

So the line of promise passed, not to the descendants of Esau, but to the DESCENDANTS OF JACOB.

THE SONS OF JACOB

It is very important to note that Jacob was NOT A JEW but he DID become the FIRST ISRAELITE.

Jacob's name was changed from Jacob to 'Israel' at Peniel and his sons became 'the children of Israel'.

All the 'promises' made to Abraham and Isaac were now vested in Jacob.

Jacob had twelve sons:

Jacob (Israel)

- Reuben (the firstborn to whom the promise **should** have gone)
- Simeon
- Levi
- Judah — (Father of the House of Judah and the Jewish State of Israel)
- Issachar
- Zebulun
- Joseph — Ephraim, Manasseh: Joseph's sons
- Benjamin
- Dan
- Naphtali
- Gad
- Asher

The 'line of promise' should have gone through Reuben being the firstborn, but Jacob (Israel) decided otherwise: His son Joseph was his favourite son.

THE PROMISES PASS TO EPHRAIM AND MANASSEH

It has been commonly believed that the Jews are the sole inheritors of the promises made to the Patriarchs — THEY WERE NOT. Look as you will and you will find NO indication that the promises passed to Judah.

Her is what the Bible says about it:

> 'And Israel (Jacob) beheld Joseph's sons, and said, Who are these? And Joseph said unto his father, They are my sons, whom God hath given me in this place. And he said, Bring them I pray thee, unto me, and I will bless them.
>
> Now the eyes of Israel (Jacob) were dim from age, so that he could not see. And he brought them near unto him; and he kissed them, and embraced them.
>
> And Israel said unto Joseph, I had not thought to see thy face; and, lo, God hath shown me also thy seed.
>
> And Joseph brought them out from between his knees, and he bowed himself with his face to the earth.
>
> And Joseph took them both, Ephraim in his right hand toward Israel's left hand, and Manasseh in Israel's right hand towards Israel's left hand, and brought them near unto him.
>
> And Israel stretched out his right hand, and laid it on Ephraim's head, who was the younger, and his left hand upon Manasseh's head, guiding his hands knowingly; for Manasseh was the first born.
>
> And he blessed Joseph, and said, GOD, BEFORE WHOM MY FATHERS, ABRAHAM AND ISAAC DID WALK, THE GOD WHO FED ME ALL MY LIFE LONG UNTO THIS DAY, THE ANGEL WHO REDEEMED ME FROM ALL EVIL, BLESS THE LADS; AND LET MY NAME BE NAMED AMONG THEM, AND THE NAME OF MY FATHERS ABRAHAM AND ISAACE; AND LET THEM GROW INTO A MULTITUDE IN THE MIDST OF THE EARTH . . . AND HE BLESSED THEM THAT DAY, SAYING, GOD MAKE THEE AS EPHRAIM AND MANASSEH.' Genesis 48: Parts of verses 8-20

It is of considerable importance to our theme that the reader should note that the mainstream promises were NOT inherited by ANY of the sons of Israel but 'jumped' a generation and were passed directly to Israel's grandchildren, the sons of Joseph, Ephraim and Manasseh.

> 'Now the sons of Reuben, the firstborn of Israel for he was the firstborn; but forasmuch as he defiled his father's bed, his birthright was given unto the sons of Joseph (Ephraim and Manasseh), the sons of Israel, and the genealogy is not to be reckoned after the birthright. FOR JUDAH PREVAILED ABOVE HIS BRETHREN, AND OF HIM CAME THE PRINCE (MESSIAH); but the birthright was Joseph's.'
>
> 1.Chronicles 5:1,2

That scripture is so plain in it's meaning that it is difficult to see how so many generations of theologians have persisted in the view that the descendants of Judah are the inheritors of the promises to Israel. Only theologians of the Jewish faith, it would seem, have recognised the facts concerning the line of promise.

THE SPECIAL PROMISE TO THE HOUSE OF JUDAH

As we shall see later, the descendants of the Twelve sons of Israel became a nation and that nation existed in two 'Houses' THE HOUSE OF ISRAEL and THE HOUSE OF JUDAH.

There were three kinds of promise (1) Those made to the WHOLE nation of Israel (2) Those made specifically to the HOUSE OF ISRAEL and (3) Those made specifically to the HOUSE OF JUDAH.

It is impossible to understand the implications of the history of either ALL ISRAEL, THE HOUSE OF JUDAH or THE HOUSE OF ISRAEL unless we understand to whom the promises were made.

As I have said, there will be those who do not believe that the promises to Israel were anything other than the product of the patriarch's imagination or political guile. Certainly there will be those who will not accept that 'God' actually predestined a nation, far less that he communicated directly with them in a conversational manner as described in the Bible.

One thing that cannot be denied however, and that is why this part of our investigation is so important, is that the 'promises', whether real or imaginary, had a profound effect on the development and migration of the people of Israel. Whether or not they were actually given, and I personally having studied the evidence believe they were, the fact remains that they had as much impact on the thinking of the two houses of Israel as any proven truth has had upon any nation.

In the Genesis chapter 49 you will find the specific promises given by Israel to each of his twelve sons. It should be realised that these were not in the nature of allocations of parts of the mainline inheritance as has sometimes been believed. They were specific promises which had nothing whatsoever to do with the mainline promise which had already been given to Ephraim and Manasseh.

THE SCEPTRE AND THE LAW

For our present purpose we need only consider the special prediction of his father Israel given to Judah the father of THE HOUSE OF JUDAH.

> 'Judah, thou art he whom thy brethren shall praise: Thy hand shall be in the neck of thine enemies; thy father's children shall bow down before thee.
> Judah is a lion's whelp: from the prey, my son, thou art gone up: he stooped down, he crouched as a lion, and as an old lion. Who shall rouse him up?
> THE SCEPTRE SHALL NOT DEPART FROM JUDAH, NOR THE LAWGIVER FROM BETWEEN HIS FEET, UNTIL SHILOH (THE MESSIAH) SHALL COME; AND UNTO HIM SHALL THE GATHERING OF THE PEOPLE BE.' Genesis 49: 8-10.

That prophecy, spoken 1430 B.C. was literally fulfilled for, though THE HOUSE OF ISRAEL went into captivity in Assyria and lost her language, her identity, and her religion, THE HOUSE OF JUDAH has never lost her identity, her language or her religion.

From Judah came, as Israel (Jacob) predicted, the Messiah (Shiloh) and the Jews have remained the faithful custodians of the law to this day. We owe it to the Jews that the vast library of ancient writings is available to us, and the world cannot begin to assess the debt it owes to the greatest Jew of all.

THE DIVISION OF THE KINGDOM OF ISRAEL

Solomon was dead and King Rehoboam reigned over Israel. The HOUSE OF JUDAH and the HOUSE OF ISRAEL had existed as separately identifiable units until his reign but during his reign the two houses split into SEPARATE nations.

'So when all Israel saw that the king harkened not unto them, the people answered the king, saying, What portion have we in David? Neither have we inheritance in the son of Jesse. To your tents, O Israel, Now see to thine own house, David. So Israel departed to their tents.

But as for the children of Israel who dwelt in the cities of Judah, Rehoboam reigned over them. Then King Rehoboam sent Adoram, who was over the forced labour; and all Israel stoned him with stones, that he died. Therefore King Rehoboam made speed to get him up to his chariot, to flee to Jerusalem.

SO ISRAEL REBELLED AGAINST THE HOUSE OF DAVID UNTO THIS DAY.

And it came to pass, when all Israel heard that Jeroboam was come again, that they sent and called him into the congregation, and made him King over all Israel; THERE WAS NONE THAT FOLLOWED THE HOUSE OF DAVID, BUT THE TRIBE OF JUDAH ONLY.

And when Rehoboam was come to Jerusalem, he assembled all the house of Judah, with the tribe of Benjamin, an hundred and four-score thousand chosen men, who were warriors, to fight against the house of Israel.' 1. Kings 12: 16-24

Again this historic record is so plain as to require no interpretation. Anyone reading that passage cannot doubt that the houses of Israel and Judah had separate identities and became separate nations nor that the HOUSE OF JUDAH was composed of two tribes, the tribes of Judah and Benjamin.

From that time forth the two, the House of Israel and the House of Judah, remained separate nations. History shows that they did not come together again.

THE HOUSE OF ISRAEL GO CAPTIVE INTO ASSYRIA

The Jews dwelt in the land of Palestine as a national entity for 136 years AFTER the HOUSE OF ISRAEL was taken captive into Assyria. It is quite incorrect to speak, as some do, of THE captivity. There were SEVERAL captivities but they may be divided into two for our purpose. The HOUSE OF ISRAEL were taken captive into ASSYRIA in the year 722 B.C. and the HOUSE OF JUDAH were taken captive into BABYLON some 136 years later in 586 B.C.

The JEWS returned from their captivity in Babylon and never lost their national identity. The HOUSE OF ISRAEL suffered quite a different fate for they never returned to Palestine from their captivity in Assyria.

In the case of Judah, while they were in captivity, their land was left desolate but in the case of Israel, the Assyrians repopulated their land. Thus it was that the old territory of Israel, at the time of Christ, was populated by Samaritans.

So the KINGDOM OF ISRAEL would seem to have come to it's 'end' in the year 722 B.C., taken captive by Tilgarpileser, the king of Assyria. From that time forth, even unto our day, the millions of people forming the ten-tribed House of Israel have been 'lost'.

Until the last hundred years or so historians have been content to accept the disappearance of the major part of the nation of Israel without question. Though, to their credit, the Jews have always kept alive the knowledge of their 'missing' brethren.

IN SEARCH OF THE MISSING MILLIONS

Writing in the first century A.D. the Jewish historian, Josephus, had seemed to close the book on the history of the House of Israel when he wrote:

> 'The ENTIRE BODY of the people of Israel; remained in that country; wherefore there are but two tribes (Judah and Benjamin) in Asia and Europe subject to the Romans, while the ten tribes are beyond the Euphrates till now, and are an immense multitude not to be estimated by numbers. Book XI

So we know that the ENTIRE BODY of the ten tribes of Israel were still intact in Josephus' day over eight hundred years AFTER they had been taken into captivity. We know they were an IMMENSE MULTITUDE in the first century A.D.

> As far back as 1879 the JEWISH CHRONICLE stated: 'The Scriptures speak of the future restoration of Israel, which is clearly to include both Judah and Ephraim. The problem then is reduced to it's simplest form. THE TEN TRIBES ARE CERTAINLY IN EXISTENCE. All that has to be done is to discover which people represent them.'

When Dr. Herts, in 1918 Chief Rabbi of the British Empire, was asked his views on the composition of the Jewish people, he replied: 'The people at present known as Jews are the descendants of the tribes of Judah and Benjamin, with a certain number of the descendants of the tribe of Levi. So far as is known there is not any further admixture of the tribes.'

It would seem to be only gentile theologians who are in any doubt about the fact that THE HOUSE OF JUDAH and THE HOUSE OF ISRAEL have separate existences.

Is it yet another coincidence that we can trace the origins of the early Brythons from the very area in which the ten tribes of Israel disappeared?

WHAT'S IN A NAME?

It is, of course, a mistake to search the records of history for a people by the name of Israel. Undoubtedly the Assyrians would not call them by that name and we would not therefore expect to find them by that name in Assyrian records.

We in the English speaking world do not call the German homeland Deutschland, we call it Germany. Anyone who has watched international events on television will know that people of other nations do not call us British, they have their own language in which they express our nationality. In view of that is it not more than a little strange that those seeking the lost tribes of Israel have always assumed that they would find them in the pages of history as 'Israel'?

Is it not strange too that, seeking the origins of our people, historians have sought a people with the name 'British'?

The way to identify Israel in the Assyrian records is to find out what the Syrians called Israel when they took them into captivity. Of course that is not an easy process but it is a very enlightening one.

FROM THE MIDDLE EAST TO WESTERN EUROPE

My reader will have realised by now that I am proposing that the British people emanated from the nation of Israel. It is a proposition which is often met with incredulity and sometimes amusement though why it should be considered incredulous or amusing I cannot understand.

Speaking to a learned professor of history on the subject he said to me 'I find the proposition that we are the descendants of the lost tribes of Israel preposterous. I would think the lost tribes to be the Indians or the Chinese.' He could give no reason for thinking the proposition that we British are descendants of the ten lost tribes of Israel any more preposterous than his suggestion that the Indians or the Chinese are the lost tribes of Israel. Why is it more intellectually acceptable to believe the tribes are in India than to believe they are in England?

The author has found similar prejudice among theologians, many of whom seem to think that tracing the House of Israel to Britain poses some kind of threat to their theology. Theologians who will quite happily speculate that the House of Israel is to be found in all kinds of exotic places consider the identification of Britain with the House of Israel as being almost heresy.

We commenced our investigation into the origins of the English speaking peoples because we were impressed by those things which were common between the Israelitish faith in Palestine and the Druid faith in Britain. We began with a link between the Middle East and Britain. It is evident from the 'Dictionary of Word Origins' that the English language originated in the Middle East. There is therefore enough evidence for us to continue to pursue our enquiry.

THE APOCRYPHA AS HISTORY

There is some further evidence as to the migration of the ten tribed HOUSE OF ISRAEL to be found in the Apocrypha. It should be remembered that, though the church has largely disallowed the use of the Apocrypha for use in determining doctrinal matters it is still widely regarded as being accurate from a historical point of view. Jesus would have taught from the Septuagint, which included the books we now call the Apocrypha.

Esdras, as recorded in the Apocrypha, throws more light on the migrations of the HOUSE OF ISRAEL:

> 'These are the ten tribes, which were led away out of their own land in the time of Osea the king, whom Salmanasar the king of the Assyrians led away captive, and he carried them beyond the river, and they were carried into another land. And they entered by the narrow passages of the river Euphrates. For the Most High then wrought signs for them, and stayed the springs of the river, till they were passed over. For through that country there was a great way to go, namely, of a year and a half: and the same region is called Arzareth. Then dwelt they there until the latter time.'
>
> 2 Esdras 13: 40-48

That tells us the Assyrians placed the captive Israelites in two separate areas, the first being the Gozan and river Habur area in Assyria and the second in what is now known as Northern Iran.

We do not know the date of which Esdras was writing but as he wrote about 541 B.C. and the House of Israel went into captivity in 722 B.C. it must have been between those two dates.

THE RUSSIAN EVIDENCE

The tribes were, Esdras tells us, crossing the Euphrates in the direction of Europe and had to travel about a year and a half's journey. Even allowing for the slowness with which such a mass of people would move on foot and the skirmishes they would meet on the way there is little doubt that journeying for that length of time in that direction they would have reached Britain.

If the assumption that the tribes journeyed in the direction of Britain is correct then they would have passed through the Caucasus, the Black Sea and the Crimea. Thence they would have moved into central Europe and onward to the North Sea coasts of Europe.

There should be SOME evidence of people of Hebrew origin passing through — and there is!

The Russian professor Chwolson had knowledge of over seven hundred tombstones which were discovered in the Crimea proving that Israel was there. He also examined one hundred and fifty epigrams of great antiquity found in Hebrew burial places.

Quoting from BRITISH HISTORY TRACED FROM EGYPT AND PALESTINE, F. Wallace Cannon tells of some of them:

> 'This is the tombstone of Buki, the son of Izchak, the priest. May his rest be in Eden at the time of the salvation of Israel. In the year 702 of the years of our exile'
> 'Rabbi Moses Levi, died in the year 726 of our exile.'
> 'Zadok, the Levite, son of Moses, died 4000 after the creation, 785 of our exile.'
> So there is no doubt from a factual standpoint that at least some members of the tribes of Israel migrated westwards towards central Europe.

We now see that not only do the British enjoy the link of language with the ancient Middle East, there is too the link of religion and the link of the tombstones.

Further evidence is to be found in the fact that a brooch of the Celtic/Pict design was found in an Egyptian tomb. The usual flow of migration from east to west would suggest that the Celtic design came from the East with it's originators rather than that it emanated from the Celts of Europe.

A rich cache of jewellery with typical Celtic zoomorphic decoration was found on St. Ninians Island and a similar collection of jewellery with similar decoration was found shortly afterwards in the area of the Caspian Sea.

In her excellent book 'The Celtic Influence', published by The Covenant Publishing Company, Gladys Taylor writes:

> 'George Bain, the supreme specialist on Celtic design, whose own patterns were based, very effectively, upon the methods used by the designers of Celtic jewellery and manuscripts, studied the history of all related crafts very closely indeed. In an article in the magazine 'Scotland' published in 1934, he summed up his findings in these words "Influences upon Celtic art are to be found in Eastern Siberia and throughout Russia and the whole of northern Europe and along the great rivers leading to the Caspian Sea and the Black Sea, wherever the waves of the migrating northern people found passage and substance for themselves and their animals, centuries before Greece became a nation."
>
> Gladys Taylor comments:
>
> 'It is surely more than coincidence that metal workers in places thousands of miles apart should have been using identical methods; apart from the remote possibility of British craftsmen sending such a quantity of goldwork to that distant region in the Middle East, the only conclusion is that the craftsmen themselves MIGRATED FROM EAST TO WEST, bringing their skills and practising them in all the regions of their settlement.'

Let us look again at the things we know so far. We know that the larger part of Israel were taken from their own land by the Assyrians and went into captivity in the region of Media the other side of the great River Euphrates from Palestine. We know that there was a considerable migration from that region but that there was still a vast people 'not to be numbered' the other side of the Euphrates at the time of Christ. We know that the earlier migration headed for a destination 'one and a half year's journey' away from Media and that that length of journey would take them to the limits of the then known world — Britain. We have seen that archaeology attests to Israelites travelling along the route the tribes of Israel would have had to travel to reach Britain.

This all throws new light on the proposition that the Virgin Mary lived for many years, died and was buried, in England. What would be more natural than, if Jesus and Mary wished, or had to, travel abroad, they would come to dwell among people of their own nation who had migrated here hundreds of years before?

At the time of Jesus, the migrations of the tribes of Israel to these isles had not finished, it would continue for hundreds of years with other tribes in later invasions joining the original Brythons and Celts. Several hundred years AFTER the time of Jesus the last of the captive Israelites mentioned by Josephus were to start their long trek across Europe to join with their brothers already settled in the isles. There is evidence to suggest that the various 'invasions' of this country from the continent were different tribes of the same origin 'coming home'. The stragglers of the ten tribes filtering into these islands from the continent hundreds of years after the vanguard of the Israelitish occupation had arrived.

THE MYSTERY OF THE NAME

As I have mentioned the people of one nation often have a different name for another nation from the one by which that nation knows itself. We find Norway spoken of as 'Norge', Germany as 'Deutschland' and, even in our small group of islands the Welsh refer to Wales as 'Cymru'.

The tribes of Israel were taken captive into Assyria but we must not expect them to appear by that name in the Assyrian archives.

Fortunately there are, in the British Museum, documents from the archives of Nineveh which date back to the reign of Esarhaddon, king of Assyria (about 680 B.C.) which tell us much about Assyria at that time. At about the time the Israelites were taken captive there appears in the archives a new national name which one can only assume was one of the names by which the Assyrians called the newly captured Israelites, the new name was 'Scythians'.

We know that the Assyrians also called the Israelites 'Khumri' or 'Gimiri', which does not seem so far from the present day Welsh name for Wales 'Cymru'!

Israel was known to the Assyrians as Beth-Khumri, 'Beth' meaning 'the people of' and Khumri being the Assyrian corruption of the king of Israel's name 'Omri'. On the Black Obelisk in the British Museum there is an inscription recording 'The tribute of Jehu, son of Khumri'. The inscription predates the captivity of Israel by over a century showing that the Israelites were known as 'Khumri' by the Assyrians long before they became captives.

That the Scythians left Media between 620 B.C. and 600 B.C. is beyond doubt. The Assyrian power collapsed in 609 B.C and Nineveh fell in 612 B.C The Medes did not have the Assyrian enthusiasm for playing host to the Israelitish hordes which by that time had become more allies of the Assyrians than captives.

The only course left open to the Scythians would be to escape northwards and into Russia via the Dariel Pass through the Caucasus mountains.

From there we can follow the trail of Scythian tombs (dating from 580 B.C.) into Europe.

It used to be thought that the Scythians had migrated into Europe from central Asia but in 'Treasures from Scythian Tombs' M.I. Artamov of Leningrad writes:

> 'In the animal style so typical of Scythian art, the figures of the animals in the oldest examples are of Near Eastern derivation. The compositions with the tree of life, seen in the gold settings of the swords from both Kelermes and the Melgunov treasure, not only reproduce an ancient Mesopotamian subject, but in no way differ stylistically from similar Assyrian and Urartian designs.'

So we sec that the Scythians and the Khumbri were first mentioned in Assyrian literature about the time Israel were taken captive into Assyria and we can trace their migration from Assyria into Central Europe.

THE SCOTS HAVE ALWAYS KNOWN THEY WERE OF SCYTHIAN ORIGIN

It would seem that awareness of our Scythian ancestry has only recently been lost, for in 1316 the Scots appealed to the Pope in the 'Declaration of Arbroath' in the following terms:

> 'We know, Most Holy Father and Lord, and from the chronicles and books of the ancients gather, that among other illustrious nations, ours, to wit, the nation of the Scots, has been distinguished by many honours; which PASSING FROM THE GREATER SCYTHIA through the Mediterranean Sea and the Pillar of Hercules (Gibraltar), and sojourning in Spain among the most savage tribes through a long course of time, could nowhere be

> subjugated by any people however barbarous; and coming thence ONE THOUSAND TWO HUNDRED YEARS AFTER THE OUTGOING OF THE PEOPLE OF ISRAEL, they, by many victories and infinite toil, acquired for themselves the possessions of the West which they now hold, after EXPELLING THE BRITONS and completely destroying the Picts, and, although very often assailed by the Norwegians, the Danes and the English, always kept themselves free from all servitude . . .'

An even earlier link with the Middle East is established in the 'Legend of Brandon'

> 'Now one of the sons of Gaythelos, Hyber by name, a young man but valiant for his years, being incited to war by his spirit, took up arms, and having prepared such a fleet as he could, went to the aforesaid island, and slew part of the inhabitants he found, and part he subdued. He thus appropriated the whole land as a possession for himself and his brethren, calling it SCOTIA from his mother's name.'

Who was Scotia from whom, it would appear, Scotland got it's name? She was the daughter of Pharoah. She and her husband Gaythelos were expelled from Egypt soon after the Exodus of Israel. The fact that her son Hyber claimed and named Scotland is significant for the word 'Hibernian' is still dear to Scottish hearts.

It is not the purpose of this book to PROVE that the British race are the descendants of the Ten Lost Tribes of Israel and the author would not at all suggest that he has done so here. There are other able works however that, in the author's opinion DO prove that the English speaking people originated in the land of ancient Israel. Many religious conclusions have been drawn from that fact but it is not the purpose of this book to stress them beyond saying that it would undoubtedly have had a considerable bearing upon the fact that the Virgin Mary and Jesus would indeed have made it a priority, as he said, to come to 'The lost sheep of the House of Israel'.

11 The Reign Of Terror

It was very early in the ministry of Jesus that the Sanhedrin instituted fear of excommunication from the synagogue as a weapon in their armoury against Jesus (John 9-22).

To be excommunicated from a religious order may seem to be a trivial thing to us today, but in Palestine in those days it meant almost total social ostracism.

That terror reigned among the followers, friends and close relatives of Jesus is obvious from the record of his trial and crucifixion. The howling of the lynch mob 'crucify him, crucify him' can be heard echoing through the hollow caverns of time. Yet before that, at the time of his arrest we are told 'Then all the disciples forsook him, and fled.' Matthew 26:56.

Considering that the disciples were mainly family and close friends we can only imagine what news had come to their ears about the hatred which threatened to overwhelm their master and his cause. We have either to think of them as cowards or accept that they knew that a persecution of Gestapo-like intensity was about to break over them.

What else can explain the fact that, apart from Joseph of Arimathea and a few other Sanhedrin stalwarts, all of them men who by reason of their positions in the Sanhedrin were beyond the threat of immediate persecution, none of Jesus' followers were at the trial?

How else can we explain the magnitude of Peter's about-face? This man who, but a short while before, had triumphantly proclaimed 'Thou art the Christ, the Son of the Living God' and to whom Jesus had replied 'Blessed art thou, Simon Barjona; for flesh and blood hath not revealed it unto thee, but my Father, who is in heaven', denied Jesus three times before two serving wenches and a crowd of onlookers.

> 'Now Peter sat outside in the court, and a maid came unto him, saying, Thou also wast with Jesus of Galilee. But he denied it before them all, saying, I know not what thou sayest. And when he

was gone out into the porch another maid saw him, and said unto them that were there, This fellow was also with Jesus of Nazareth. And again he denied with an oath, I do not know the man. And after a while came unto him they that stood by, and said to Peter, Surely thou also art one of them; for thy speech betrayeth thee. Then began he to curse and to swear, saying, I know not the man.'

You can almost feel Peter's terror coming through the record. Had there not been inpending persecution of the followers of Jesus why should Peter have denied Jesus with such vehemence as to cause him to 'curse and swear'? Why else would this man who but a few months before had been prepared to use the sword against the High Priest become so seemingly cowardly?

The absence of the disciples of Jesus from the trial and their failure to give him help or comfort in the hours prior to the crucifixion is disgraceful if there was not good reason for their desertion. Men have been burned at the stake rather than deny their Lord and yet here we see the band of close relatives and friends so deserting him that a stranger, a Cyrene by the name of Simon was forced to carry Jesus' cross for him. We can only assume that the hunt was on for the close disciples of Jesus even before he was dead, a hunt which was designed to eradicate the memory of Jesus from the annals of history.

The intensity of the hatred against Jesus is to be seen from the facts of his trial, which trial was, as we have seen, illegal under Jewish law. Yet it was thought so important by them, to rid themselves of Jesus that the trial of Jesus was manipulated by those who prided themselves on being, and usually were, the custodians of the law. It is to be seen too from the fact that the Sanhedrin, not the Romans as is so often erroniously taught, put a guard on the tomb where Jesus' body was laid.

THE GUARD ON THE TOMB

In passing it is well to observe that those who dismiss the resurrection with the argument that Jesus did not really die but survived the cross, and was later revived and walked from the tomb, have little understanding of the depth of hatred and suspicion which sent Jesus to his death.

How can we think that a Sanhedrin which was so full of antipathy and fear that it chose to break it's own sacred laws to put Jesus to death would not make sure that Jesus was dead? It was because they remembered that Jesus had said he would rise again on the third day that they were prepared to put a guard on his tomb. Being aware of the impending resurrection, or plot to simulate a resurrection, would they have allowed Jesus to be buried before they had made sure that he was actually dead? The proposition requires more credulity than belief in the resurrection does!

> 'Now the next day, that followed the day of the preparation, the chief priests and the Pharisees came together unto Pilate, saying, Sir, WE REMEMBER that that deceiver said, while he was yet alive, After three days I will rise again. Command, therefore, that the sepulchre be made sure until the third day, lest his disciples come by night, and steal him away, and say unto the people, He is risen from the dead; so the last error shall be worse than the first.'
> Matthew 27: 62-64.

Can we imagine such cautious people NOT making sure that Jesus was dead?

It is interesting, in passing, to note that, after the resurrection we never read of them calling Jesus 'that deceiver' again! Though the Sanhedrin persecuted the Disciples for preaching the resurrection and tried to stop them doing so, they never once denied it as a fact. One imagines they knew rather more about the facts than some of our present day bishops.

The cauldron of persecution was already bubbling when Jesus was laid to rest in the tomb and it was to break forth in dreadful ferocity after the resurrection.

We have already seen that the Jewish Hierarchy's disagreement with Jesus was no mere intellectual disagreement but an all consuming hatred akin to the Nazi hatred of the Jews during the Second World War. This is shown in sharp relief in the martyrdom of Stephen.

JUDGE BITES PRISONER!

Stephen was brought before the High Priests and the Council and astonishing scenes of hatred ensued. 'When they heard these things, they were cut to the heart, and they gnashed on him with their teeth'. The word translated 'gnashed' is 'brucho' and means 'bit'.

Can you imagine the dignified and somewhat pompous members of the council becoming so filled with hatred they descended to actually biting someone who was being examined before the council? THAT is the kind of hatred that filled the hearts of the people who opposed the Gospel of Jesus Christ! Could the Virgin Mary have remained in a land where there was THAT degree of hatred?

The story of how Stephen was stoned to death is too familiar to require reiteration but there is a verse at the beginning of chapter eight of the Acts of the Apostles which tells us of the persecution of the church after the resurrection of Jesus:

> 'And Saul consented to his (Stephen's) death. And at that time there was a great persecution against the church which was at Jerusalem; and they were ALL SCATTERED ABROAD throughout the regions of Judea and Samaria, except the apostles.'
>
> At the beginning of chapter nine we read:
>
> 'And Saul, yet breathing out threatenings and slaughter against the disciples of the Lord, went unto the high priest, and desired of him letters to Damascus to the synagogues, that if he found any of this way, whether they were men or women, he might bring them bound unto Jerusalem.'

There was no hidding place for Christians, either men or women in the Holy Land. Obviously the Virgin Mary, Joseph of Arimathea and their companions were at risk of being imprisoned or being put to death. We know that ALL the disciples other than the apostles dispersed — that MUST incude Mary and her companions because they were NOT apostles.

THE PRIME TARGETS OF SAUL'S HATRED

Of all the people who Saul would be pursuing none would be more vulnerable than Mary the mother of Jesus for she was a living testimony to the virgin birth and the events of the resurrection morning. Joseph of Arimathea who had buried the body was able to testify to the fact that Jesus HAD, in fact, been dead when he laid him in the tomb and could testify too, to the fact of the empty tomb. The women who had discovered the empty tomb and spoken with the resurrected Christ would also have been prime targets.

Is it reasonable to assume that ALL that were 'scattered abroad' did NOT include Mary and Joseph? Is it at all reasonable to believe that, of all Jesus' followers, Saul of Tarsus would have allowed Mary the Mother of Jesus to live either in, or in the lands around Palestine? The very word 'all' is so inclusive as to demand the interpretation that only the apostles did not flee before the wrath of Saul and that Joseph of Arimathea and the Virgin

Mary did not remain in Palestine. Since Saul's intention was to destroy the faith all REASON demands that the Virgin Mary would not be allowed to remain. If she did not remain — then where had they gone?

WHO WAS THE VIRGIN MARY'S GUARDIAN AFTER THE CRUCIFIXION

Who was Mary's guardian after the crucifixion? We find the answer in John 19:27 'Then saith he (Jesus) to the disciple (John), Behold thy mother! And from that hour that disciple took her unto his own [home].' The word 'home' is not in the original and of course it changes the meaning. 'He took her unto his own' is the correct rendering. At the time John was a hunted man and the only interpretation is that he took Mary to his own family.

Jowett in his DRAMA OF THE LOST DISCIPLES, published by The Covenant Publishing Company, quotes from Magna Glastoniensis Tabula 'St. John, while evangelising Ephesus, made Joseph Paranymphos.' A 'Paranymphos' was of course a guardian. He goes on 'We read in pp. 42 and 71, the statement that St. John and St. Joseph were alone called 'Paranymphos' to the Blessed Virgin. The COTTON. MS. TITUS also relates the same facts. British testimony is supplied by Capgrave.

So the two men responsible for the safety and well-being of the Virgin Mary were the apostle John and Joseph of Arimathea.

One thing is certain, Mary could not have stayed with John or any of the apostles for they were hunted men.

The Roman Empire sprawled across the face of Europe. Tiberius proclaimed an edict, later perpetuated by Claudius that it was an offence to be a Christian. Where could the Mary band go, certainly not to any territory governed by Rome!

ADRIFT IN AN OPEN BOAT

Joseph of Arimathea, being an influential Roman official would be untouchable by Saul until Rome itself became anti-Christian. Undoubtedly he would, at first, have been in a position to help the women to escape imprisonment or death but as the Roman attitude to Christianity hardened Saul would recognise that he had the opportunity to purge Palestine of it's most dangerous Christian element — the family of Jesus.

The hatred which led to Saul's participation in the death of Stephen in A.D. 33, the year of Jesus' resurrection, had, three years later festered, and in A.D. 36 had driven him to mount a massive persecution, probing deep into Roman territory to hunt out the scattered Christians. Those who had fled to Judea and Samaria had been hunted down or had fled further afield.

There is a silence from the writers of the gospels about what happened to the vulnerable relations of Jesus. Why does that silence exist? It would be strange if it did not exist for the writers of the gospels were hunted men and doubtless had no contact with either the mother of Jesus, Joseph of Arimathea or the witnesses to the resurrection. The apostles would have HEARD later what had happened to Mary and Joseph but they were not inclined to report hearsay.

Tradition has it that the following fourteen were set adrift in a boat without oars or sails:

Mary, wife of Cleopas,
Salome and her maid,
Mary Magdalene,
Martha and her maid,
Lazarus,
Joseph of Arimathea,
Trophimus,
Maximin,
Cleon,
Eutropius,
Sidonius,
Martial, and
Saturninus.

In his excellent book THE COMING OF THE SAINTS J. W. Taylor writes:

> 'There is no doubt that this tradition, much as is given in the LIFE OF RABANUS, was accepted by the whole Latin Church for over a thousand years. For proof of this we only have to turn to the Breviary at St. Martha's Day, July 29th. There we find a lection for the second nocturne which tells how Mary, Martha and Lazarus with their servant Marcella, and Maximin, one of the Seventy-two disciples, were seized by the Jews, placed in a boat without sails or oars, and carried safely to the port of Marseilles. Moved by this remarkable fact, the people of the neighbouring lands were speedily converted to Christianity; Lazarus became bishop of Marseilles, Maximinus of Aix, Mary lived and died an anchoress on a high mountain of those parts, while Martha founded

a convent of women, died on the fourth day before the kalends of August, and was buried with great honour at Tarascon.'

Mr. Taylor also quotes from Roger de Hovedon (730-1200):

> 'Marseilles is an episcopal city under the domination of the King of Arragon. Here are the relics of St. Lazarus, the brother of St. Mary Magdalene and Martha, who held the bishopric here for seven years after Jesus restored him from the dead.'

Why is there no record there of Joseph of Arimathea? Because, as tradition tells us, Joseph did not stay in France, he travelled on to Glastonbury. Why should French tradition say that? Surely, if the traditions are superstitious inventions the one person the French would have been delighted to 'keep' would have been the man who buried the body of Jesus and who is reputed to have had in his possession the Holy Grail.

DID THE VIRGIN MARY TRAVEL INCOGNITO?

Why is there no record of the Virgin Mary in the boat or at Marseilles? Would Mary have been so important to Saul that she had to be brought aboard without his, or anyone's knowledge? Had Joseph got her out of Palestine before on one of his ships to England. The only proposition that does NOT stand up is that she remained behind in Palestine.

John and Joseph of Arimathea had been appointed guardians of the Virgin Mary, John was on the run, terror was everywhere. Can we even consider that her uncle, Joseph, would have left her to face almost certain imprisonment and possible death? It is unthinkable! She may have travelled anonymously, perhaps it was she who travelled disguised as Marcella the maid. It is interesting to note that the maid Sarah was not taken in the boat until she threw herself in the sea as it was leaving and at Salome's insistence was brought into the boat. Why was one maid in the boat from the beginning and the other maid seemingly not invited? It is not to be expected that the women would be encouraged to take maids on such a voyage.

It would certainly have been a sensible thing to do to keep the identity of Mary hidden for, of all people, she would be the prime target, not only of Saul but of anyone along the way who was less than sympathetic to Christianity. As a 'maid' Mary would have been relatively safe.

The last we read of Mary the mother of Jesus in Palestine is that she was gathered together with the disciples in the Upper Room on the Day of Pentecost. Since she was one of those endued with that miraculous power from on high, why do we not read about her again in the Acts of the Apostles? Where was she? Had Joseph, anticipating the coming persecution, arranged for her to leave Palestine on one of his ships? It is possible if Joseph considered himself and Mary to be in grave danger.

Only the most extenuating circumstances would have caused a Jewish guardian to let his charge out of his sight. Guardianship was a sacred duty in the Jewish faith and we can be sure that Joseph did his duty well. If Joseph WAS in the kind of danger that forced him to send Mary away on one of his ships then we can be sure he had a trusted captain.

I am inclined to the view that the Virgin Mary travelled with Joseph in the boat when it was set adrift, disguised as one of the servants, the servant 'Marcella', and that is the reason why only ONE servant was actually taken onto the boat and the other taken on only after she had thrown herself into the water and presumably threatened to drown herself. How else can we explain Salome not taking HER maid, who was obviously desirous of going, when another servant was already on board?

So that was the situation in A.D. 36. The two 'guardians' of the Virgin Mary had been caught up in a terrible persecution and John was a wanted man. Both he and Joseph must, if Mary was in Palestine during that time, have feared for her safety. All Mary's close associates and friends, the women who had been at Calvary with her, the women who had gone to the empty tomb with her and her guardian uncle had been set adrift in a boat without cars or sails on the Mediterranean sea. Can we really believe that Mary stayed in Palestine? When Joseph and his companions were set adrift in the oarless boat there had been no record of the Virgin Mary having been in Palestine for almost three years.

12 The British Royal Gift To Joseph Of Arimathea

We have established that it is unlikely that the Virgin Mary could safely remain in Palestine for very long after the onset of the great persecution. It was soon after that that the priests declared open war on Christianity. (Acts 4). We know too that Joseph of Arimathea became the sole guardian of the Virgin Mary when the task of looking after her became impossible for John to perform due to his being caught up in the persecution which descended on the church in those early days after the resurrection of Jesus.

When we ask why there is no mention of the mother of Jesus after the brief mention in Acts Chapter 1, just over a month after Jesus' death, the question demands an answer. Are we to believe that she, Joseph of Arimathea, Lazarus and the women who were so dear to Jesus played no further part in the propagation of the gospel of Jesus? Are we to assume that in trying to wipe out every trace of Christianity the Jews, and the Romans, overlooked altogether the most dangerous people of all, Mary who gave birth to the Messiah, the influential Joseph of Arimathea who buried Jesus in his own grave, Lazarus who was raised from the dead by Jesus and the women who had been witnesses to the empty tomb? To make such an assumption would be extraordinary indeed!

However, we must admit, the assumption that Mary was not in Palestine does not prove that she was in England though the assumption must be that she was either with, or had been sent somewhere by, her guardian. There can be little doubt that, whether Joseph had SENT her or travelled with her, he would wish to join her at the first opportunity.

THE VULNERABILITY OF THE VIRGIN MARY

Though the disciples and the early church did not accord Mary the veneration which is common in modern Catholicism neither did it withhold from her the due deference which modern Protestantism is prone to withhold. The disciples would have not forgotten the 'Magnificat' of the

Virgin Mary:

If we contemplate the Virgin Mary as a real person rather than a religious myth, we begin to think of her in a new perspective and many questions come to mind. She did not exist in a vacuum! Mary, apart from her high calling, was an ordinary woman who was vulnerable to all the things to which we are vulnerable. If we accept Mary as a real person we will not for one moment contemplate the thought that she would live in the wholly hostile land of Palestine after Joseph had left nor would she go to live in a distant land without someone she knew being with her.

Where was Mary? We know where her friends were. The disciples of Jesus were scattered abroad, the apostles were under threat of imprisonment and death, her women friends were in the boat adrift on the Mediterranean and Joseph was with them. When everyone else had fled or been banished, is it reasonable to assume that Mary would remain?

We have seen why, if she was not in Palestine, there was only one country in the world to which she would have easy access and probably also have friends among the people who knew her uncle. If the traditions are true that she had come here with Jesus then she would possibly have many friends herself who would welcome her here.

We would also expect there to be a Christian church in Britain at a very early date because we would not believe that Joseph of Arimathea, Mary and other disciples would come here without spreading the Christian message.

Of course, anyone who accepts that St. Augustine brought Christianity to Britain will find it difficult to comprehend how either Joseph or the Virgin Mary would come to live in a land of heathen 'painted savages'. However it is a well attested fact that St. Augustine was NOT the first to bring Christianity to Britain.

Where would Mary go after she left Palestine? The obvious answer would seem to be that she would go to a place where the Patriarchal religion was practised and where the faith of her son was accepted. The ONE place in the world where the name of her son had been revered for hundreds of years before it had even been HEARD in Palestine.

The facts are that our ancestors in A.D. 33-36 were highly civilised and already had a Christian Church here, the first Christian Church in the world. The name of Jesus was already worshipped here and there was already a family business in existence in these isles. Britain would seem to be the sensible choice for Mary in her exile.

THE WORLD'S FIRST CHRISTIAN CHURCH

If I were to ask my readers where the first Christian church existed, most would say 'Jerusalem' and some would say 'Rome' but both would be wrong. The first Christian church existed in Britain, according to tradition, built by the hands of Jesus himself.

Even if we do not accept THAT tradition there is still evidence that there was no more than a short lapse between the date of the establishment of the first Christian church in Jerusalem and the establishment of the first Christian church in these islands. What cannot be denied is that the first Christian church in the world, outside of Jerusalem, was the THE BRITISH CHURCH. It is however important that we do not confuse THE BRITISH CHURCH with the CHURCH OF ENGLAND.

In Jerusalem the 'church', by which I mean that mystical body of Christ, met together informally to 'break bread' but continued 'Daily with one accord in the Temple' and in the Synagogues (Acts 2:46). Their meetings were in the houses of the 'members' and it is not until later that we read of anything like a church organisation coming into being.

THE CHURCH IN ROME EVANGELISED BY MISSIONARIES FROM BRITAIN

It is often thought that St. Paul was responsible for taking Christianity to Rome but that is not so. The church in Rome existed before St. Paul went to Rome and the evidence is that it spread to Rome not from Palestine but from Britain. In fact, at the time Christianity took root in Britain, the Apostle Paul (then Saul of Tarsus) was yet 'breathing out threatenings and slaughter' against the Christian Faith. He was yet to encounter the glorified Christ on the road to Damascus.

We know Christianity reached Rome in the early days of the church, but Rome did not become Christian until the late sixth century A.D. and Roman evangelism did not commence in Britain until St. Augustine. Though it is true to say that St. Augustine brought Roman Catholicism to Britain, it is not true to say he brought Christianity to Britain as we shall see.

One of the most profound indications of the early coming of the saints to these islands is the fact that a strong Christian church is known to have existed here immediately after the resurrection.

R. W. Morgan writes:

> 'Christianity was first introduced into Britain by Joseph of Arimathea, A.D. 36-39; followed by Simon Zelotes, the apostle; then by Aistobulus, the first bishop of the Britons; then by St. Paul. Its first converts were members of the royal family of Siluria — that

is, Gladys, the sister of Caradog, Gladys (Claudia) and Eurgen his daughters, Linus his son, converted in Britain before they were carried into captivity to Rome. The two cradles of Christianity in Britain were Ynys Wydrin, 'the Crystal Isle,' translated by the Saxons Glastonbury, in Somersetshire, where Joseph settled and taught, and Siluria, where the earliest churches and schools, next to Ynys Wydrin, were founded by the Silurian dynasty.'

So the traditions come together (a) That Joseph of Arimathea and his companions were set adrift in a boat and landed at Marseilles (b) That certain of his band became based in Marseilles and the surrounding area though they did visit Britain (c) That Joseph of Arimathea established the first Christian church outside of Jerusalem at Glastonbury.

ROMAN CATHOLIC TESTIMONY TO THE BRITISH CHURCH BEING THE FIRST CHURCH IN THE WORLD

Why, we must ask, has not the antiquity of THE BRITISH CHURCH been recognised before now? Ah, but it has! As we have seen St. Augustine, often put forward as the first missionary to the British, recognised it and informed his Pope of it.

Many authorative sources testify to the antiquity of the British Church. Polydore Vergil lived and pursued his distinguished career in the reign of Henry VII attested to the fact. He was proxy Bishop of Bath and Wells, a parish only a few miles from Glastonbury, Prebendary of Brent and Wells Cathedral and Archdeacon of Wells.

Vergil was born in Italy in 1470, studied at Bologna and Padua and became Chamberlain to Pope Alexander VII. Henry VII asked him to write an English History, so renowned were his literary talents. We might observe that as an Italian and a Catholic Vergil had no axe to grind on behalf of Britain or the British Church. It would have suited him much better if he could have written of Rome as being the mother Church but he could not and did not. He wrote:

> 'Britain, partly through Joseph of Arimathea, partly through Fugatus and Damianus, was of all kingdoms FIRST TO RECEIVE THE GOSPEL.'

During the Reign of Queen Mary, Cardinal Pole (A.D. 1555), affirmed in the presence of Mary and Phillip before the Lords and Commons in the great Chamber at Whitehall.

> 'The See Apostolic from whence I come hath a special respect to this realm above all others, and not without cause, seeing that God Himself, as it were, by providence hath given to this realm prerogative of nobility above all others, which to make plain unto you, IT IS TO BE CONSIDERED THAT THIS ISLAND FIRST OF ALL ISLANDS RECEIVED THE LIGHT OF CHRIST'S RELIGION.'
>
> Pole was, of course, a dedicated Roman Catholic.

The following day, speaking in Westminster Abbey before Phillip, Mary and the assembled Lords and Commons, Cardinal Pole said:

> 'Once again God hath given a token of His special favour to the realm, for as this nation in the time of the Primitive Church was the first to be called out of the darkness of heathenism, so now they are the first to whom God has given grace to repent of their schism'
>
> Genebrard wrote:
>
> 'The glory of Britain, consists not only in this, that she was the first country which in a national capacity publicly professed herself Christian, but that she made this confession when the Roman Empire was PAGAN AND A CRUEL PERSECUTOR OF CHRISTIANITY.'

When the antiquity of the British church was challenged by the ambassadors of France and Spain before the Roman Catholic Council of Pisa (A.D. 1417), the British delegates Robert Hallam, Bishop of Salisbury, Henry Chichele, a former Archbishop of Canterbury and Thomas Chillendon, won the day, the council affirmed that the British church was the first Christian church.

The ambassadors appealed to the Council of Constance in A.D. 1417 and that council confirmed the findings of the Council of Pisa.

A third decision by the Council at Sienna in A.D. 1424 again confirmed the antiquity of the British church and, at the Council at Basle in 1434 it was laid down that the Churches of France and Spain had to accept the precedence of the British Church, which it was affirmed, was founded by Joseph of Arimathea 'immediately after the passion of Christ.'

The uncle of St. David, Maelgwyn of Llandaff (circa A.D. 450) wrote as follows:

> 'Joseph of Arimathea, the noble decurion, received his everlasting rest with his eleven associates in the Isle of Avalon (Glastonbury). He lies in the southern angle of the bifurcated line of the Oratorium of the Adorable Virgin. He has with him the two white vessels of silver which were filled with the blood and sweat of the great Prophet Jesus.' Cottonian MS.

> Morgan tells us:

> 'The Vatican manuscript, quoted by Baronius in his "Ecclesiastical Annals" ad annum 35 (the same year in which the Acts of the Apostles state all, except the apostles, were scattered abroad from Judea). The manuscript records that in this year Lazarus, Maria Magdalene, Martha, her handmaiden Marcella, Maximin a disciple, Joseph the Decurion of Arimathea, against all of whom the Jewish people had special reasons of emnity, were exposed to the sea in a vessel without sails or oars. The vessel drifted finally to Marseilles, and they were saved. From Marseilles Joseph and his company passed into Britain, and after preaching the Gospel there, died.'

Let us remember that this is no British folklore or tradition but a Vatican manuscript. Why should the Church of Rome wish to extol the virtues of Protestant Britain? Because it is the truth, and whatever differences may exist between the Catholic and Protestant Churches, the world owes a lot to the knowledge stored in the Vatican archives.

Again we must ask: Who was the mysterious Marcella? Why would the Jews have a special reason for emnity against a servant girl? Would the Jews not have had 'a special reason for emnity against the Virgin Mary'?

We may well quote again St. Augustine (A.D. 600) when he wrote in a letter to the Pope:

> 'In the western confines of Britain, there is a certain royal island of large extent, surrounded by water, abounding in all the beauties of nature and necessaries of life. In it the first enophites of the catholic law, God beforehand acquainted them, found a Church constructed by no human art, but by the hands of Christ Himself, for the salvation of His people. The Almighty has made it manifest by many miracles and mysterious visitations that He continues to watch over it as sacred to Himself, AND TO MARY THE MOTHER OF GOD.'

It is to be expected that wherever the mother of Jesus went the preaching of the gospel would be undertaken. The fact that the Gospel of Jesus Christ reached these islands so soon after the resurrection demands that we believe that disciples came from Jerusalem to this country soon after the resurrection. Since tradition, from many sources, nationalities and from both the Protestant and Catholic faiths are one in saying those disciples were the Arimathean Joseph's band it would be flying in the face of evidence to gainsay it.

It is understandable why Mary should leave the land of Palestine disguised, the authorities there would know that the gospel of her son would not die while she was alive. The events of that first Christmas were but forty years in the past and, undoubtedly, the events of the crucifixion and the resurrection had started people talking again about the virgin mother and her miracle child. What is less understandable is the reluctance of Joseph to declare her identity when the boat arrived at Marseilles. The others of the band seemed to have been well recieved, why not she?

IT'S A VERY SMALL WORLD!

It is not until we look at the history of those times that we realise what a very small world this world of ours was even in those days.

Though after the B.C. 54 debacle the Romans did not step ashore on these islands for another hundred years the thought was never far from their mind. Augustus, who succeeded Julius in B.C. 30 always had the thought that one day he would invade these islands. That he did not do so is a credit to the British navy which, Dion Cassius tells us, kept the Channel clear of enemy shipping. Cynvelin, the son of Caswallen who had fought Julius Caesar so well, moved his army to Dover to meet the threatened invasion, as Hitler was to do almost two thousand years later. Augustus brought over half of his disposable forces to the channel ports but remembered the cruel satire which had afflicted Julius after his failure and feared another defeat could bring him into disrepute. Augustus was not a soldier in the mould of Julius nor did he sit as securely in the Emperor's throne.

We who are used to being taught that our ancestors, at the time of the coming of the Romans were painted savages, may find it strange that, in fact, our nation was highly civilised. Cynvelin the British King was educated in Rome and was thought so highly of by Augustus Caesar that he was brought up in Caesar's Palace with Caesar's nephews.

Cynvelin became king in or about B.C. 47 and reigned until B.C. 12 when his eldest son Cuiderius (Gwyddyr) became king and Avirgus inherited the royal dukedom of Cornwall. It will come as a surprise to many people to know that there had been a British Prince resident in Rome some fifty years before Jesus was born in Bethlehem.

So the rumblings of invasion continued for almost ninety years and just ten years after Jesus had died on Calvary, seven years after it would seem the Virgin Mary took up residence at Glastonbury, the Romans came ashore again and this time they were not so easily defeated.

Joseph of Arimathea would, as an official of the Roman Government, have known of their plans and would wisely have decided discretion to be the better part of valour and have kept Mary's residence in Glastonbury in low profile.

The decision was to prove to be a wise one for five years before Joseph committed the earthly remains of Mary mother of Jesus to their last resting place (she died in A.D. 48 when she was about seventy years of age) the Romans rampaged through England. For Mary there would have been no mercy!

One of the commanders in the Roman army in Britain was none other than Titus who 22 years after the death of Mary was to destroy Jerusalem in the greatest ordeal by fire that city has ever known. The temple was destroyed and the prophecy of Jesus fulfilled 'There shall not be left here one stone upon another that shall not be thrown down'.

THE DISCIPLES AND THE KING

It is important at this point to understand the closeness which existed at that time between the British Royal family and Joseph of Arimathea. Such links are not formed overnight and would suggest that Joseph was a well respected visitor to these shores over many years before the crucifixion of Jesus.

If ever the phrase 'Wheels within wheels and cogs that are rusty' had meaning it was at the beginning of the Christian era.

We have seen how the British King Cynvelin and his brother were brought up in Rome by Augustus Caesar. Augustus liked to teach the young men of the family himself and so we have the amazing prospect of a British King having been taught, during his youth, by none other than Caesar himself.

The 'Wheel within wheels' do not end there for Cynvelin took up arms on the side of Rome and served in the German campaign under Germanicus. The friendship between Caesar and Cynvelin was to stand Britain in good stead for Cynvelin was able to persuade Caesar to reduce the heavy duties levied on the British. There was a period of 'peace in our time'.

We shall see how, later in history, the lives of the Apostle Paul, the British Prince, Linus, the Roman commander Rufus Pudens and the British Princess Gladys (daughter of Caractacus) were intertwined.

Why with all this interrelationship did the leading figures in this drama find themselves on opposite sides? Who knows? We do know however that it still happens, the relationship of our own Royal Family to the Kaiser did not stop the First World War.

A FAMILY TREE OF THE BRITISH ANCIENT ROYAL FAMILY

When Joseph of Arimathea and his companions came to Glastonbury, King Arviragus, cousin of Caractacus, granted them twelve hides of land on which no taxes were to be paid in perpetuity. Of this fact the Domesday Survey of A.D. 1088 provides confirmation 'The Domus Dei, in the great monastery in Glastingbury. This Glastingbury Church possesses in it's own villa XII hides of land which have never paid tax.'

Is that not a very strange thing for a king to do for a band of refugees? Do we not see it as being more indicative of a prior relationship, either a blood relationship, between the Virgin Mary and the British Royal Family or a close relationship between Joseph of Arimathea and the Royal Family?

Here is the 'family tree' of the ancient British Royal family A.D. 10 to A.D. 120.

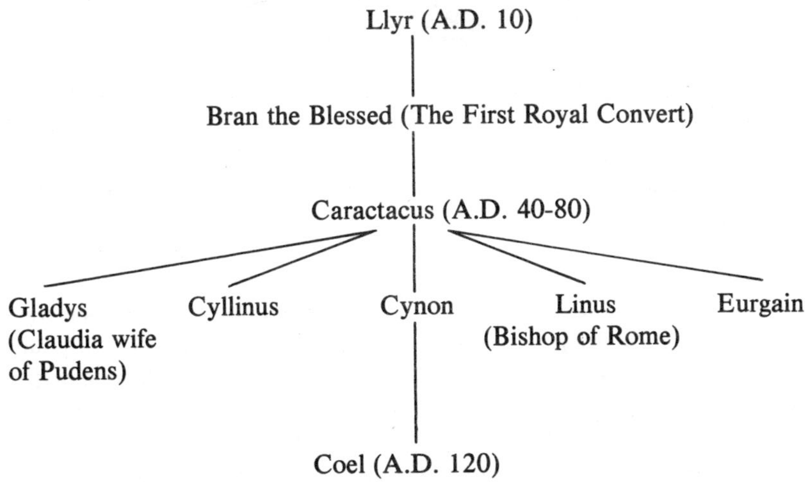

The royalty of ancient Britain are sometimes thought of as being little more than tribal leaders but that is not the case. Would Caesar have allowed Cynvelin and his brother to have been educated in his household if the boy had been nothing more than a tribesman?

Would Rufus Pudens have married Gladys, daughter of Caractacus if she had been a 'painted savage'?

Would the Roman poet, Martial, have praised her beauty and intelligence and added 'Since Claudia wife of Rufus comes from the blue-set Britons, how is it that she has won the hearts of the Latin people?' if she had been a tribeswoman?

We know the Apostle Paul to have been a highly intellectual person. Would he have written the following invitation to Rufus Pudens, his wife Claudia the British Princess, Linus the British Prince and Eubulous if the British had been tribespeople?

> 'Try to come before winter, Eubulous and Pudens, and Linus, and Claudia, and all the friends send regards to you. The Lord Jesus be with your spirit' 11. Timothy 4:21-22.

We see in that quotation, once again, the strong links between great Britain, British Royalty and the Apostles of Jesus.

WAS THE APOSTLE PAUL A HALF BROTHER TO THE ROMAN COMMANDER IN BRITAIN?

In the Epistle to the Romans Paul makes a surprising statement:

> 'Best wishes to Rufus, the chosen of the Lord, and to his and my mother.' Romans 16:13.

The only circumstance in which someone was said to be someone's mother other than their natural mother was if they received their conversion through them. This is not so of Paul. Paul's conversion on the Damascus road was by a direct revelation of Jesus by himself.

It would seem that the Apostle Paul was a half brother of the Roman Rufus Pudens and a brother-in-law of the British Princess Claudia.

THREE MILLION ROMANS TURN OUT TO SEE BRITISH KING

What of the father of Claudia and Linus, Caractacus? Was HE an unimportant and uncivilised tribal leader? Listen to him speaking in Rome after his capture and judge if this man was not as great a user of our language as Shakespeare or Churchill:

'Had my government in Britain been directed solely with the preservation of my hereditary domains, or the aggrandizement of my own family, I might long since have entered this city an ally, not a prisoner: nor would you have disdained for a friend a king descendant from illustrious ancestors, and the dictator of many nations. My present condition, stripped of it's former majesty, is as adverse to myself as it is a cause of triumph to you. What then? I was lord of men, horses, arms, wealth; what wonder if at your dictation I refused, to resign them? Does it follow that because the Romans aspire to universal domination, every nation is to accept the vassalage they would impose? I am now in your power betrayed, not conquered. Had I, like others, yielded without resistance, where would have been the name of Caradog? Where your glory? Oblivion would have buried them both in the same tomb. Bid me live. I shall survive forever in history one example at least of Roman clemency.'

Such was the fame of Caractacus that when he was taken into captivity over three million people thronged the streets of Rome to see the mighty Briton.

So well had the men of Caractacus fought that the Roman Emperor Claudius had to hasten to Britain with reinforcements, to personally take charge of the battle of Clune despite there being already three of Rome's most famous generals in the field — Aulus Plautius, Vespian, who was later to become Emperor, and Titus, the general who was to destroy Jerusalem in A.D. 70.

After the battle, Caractacus, sought shelter with the Queen of the Brigantes who betrayed him. He was taken prisoner while he slept.

Caractacus was accorded the privilege of addressing the Senate in Rome where he made the speech quoted above. The treatment Caractacus received is further evidence of the intermixing with and the closeness to the Romans of the British Royal Family. The lot of a foreign king captured by the Romans was not a happy one. Death was certain but never merciful, the ex-enemies of Rome could expect to be pulled behind chariots, disembowelled or to suffer any of a number of ghastly deaths the Romans reserved for their conquered foes.

Remember, that Caractacus was speaking to people who knew him and who knew his nation. Had anything in his speech not been fact they the Romans would have laughed him to scorn. Yet he spoke of having had:

Hereditary domains.
Being descendant from 'Illustrious ancestors'.
Being 'Dictator of many nations'.
'Former majesty'.
Having 'men, horses, arms, wealth'.

All these things, put together with the long hard struggle fought against the best commanders Rome could field, and the majestic language of Caractacus' speech show Caractacus to have been a very important king and a very well educated and articulate person — certainly no barbarian!

Caractacus remained in Rome for seven years, where he and his family lived in the 'Palace of the British'. Can we conceive for one moment that the Romans would have provided a palace for the use of a king unknown to them? There is no doubt that Caractacus had some 'pull', as our American friends would say, in Rome.

In A.D. 45 the Roman Emperor Claudius offered the hand of his daughter, Venus Julia, in marriage to the British King Arviragus and they were married in Rome. Can you imagine a Roman Emperor allowing his daughter to marry a 'painted savage'?

Far from being uncivilised tribal leaders it would seem that the Royal Family of ancient Britain were people of world renown. Put together with the fact that Jesus was surrounded by influential followers, men and women of substance (even Mary Magdelene was a rich property owner and no ordinary prostitute as some would have us believe) we see a pattern emerging. There seems little doubt that Jesus of Nazareth and his party were at thc centre of something far more international than a purely Palestinian campaign. Could THAT be why officialdom was so inordinately fearful of him?

Whatever the answer to that, one thing is certain, the closeness of the British Royal Family to the followers of Jesus Christ, Joseph of Arimathea and the Apostle Paul indicates that one has to doubt whether the relationship was some new thing. The probability increases that the Virgin Mary was of Royal blood, British Royal Blood, through her mother Anna who is said to have fled from Cornwall to Nazareth.

Why did King Aviragas grant the twelve hides of land to the Jewish refugees? Merely as a place for them to stay? Hardly! He could have done that without granting the land tax-free in perpetuity.

There would seem little doubt that the post-resurrection 'boat people' already had a considerable social standing in these islands when they stepped ashore.

13 The Wonder Of Glastonbury

There is in England, set in the rich rolling countryside of Somerset, the town and Abbey of Glastonbury. The Abbey is in ruins now but all the indications of it's former glory remain. It is well worth a visit because a holy stillness seems to pervade the ruins and the visitor is rarely left in any doubt that great and wonderful things have happened there.

It is at Glastonbury that King Aviragus granted to Joseph of Arimathea and his companions twelve hides of land which were to be tax free in perpetuity and it is at Glastonbury that the boy Jesus is said to have come with his mother and Joseph of Arimathea and have built the mud and wattle church which became known as 'Our Lady's Dowry'.

Though some, some even who accept the coming of Joseph of Arimathea to Glastonbury after the crucifixion, doubt the coming of Mary with Jesus when he was a child, the tradition is sensible enough.

If Joseph, Mary's husband, had died and Joseph of Arimathea was pursuing his business interests in Britain, it would not be unnatural if Mary had wished to see the Cornwall from which her mother had come to Palestine, nor would it be unnatural perhaps that she would wish to enquire of the whereabouts, or fate, of the father she had not seen. We may even wonder if she would have visited her royal relatives.

There is however much more evidence for the coming of Joseph of Arimathea and the Virgin Mary to Glastonbury AFTER the persecution which followed the resurrection of Jesus had made it dangerously impossible for them to live in Palestine.

In any investigation it is not good to leave the probability of how human beings would behave out of the reckoning. So let us take up the story again as the Bethany band are forced into the boat on the shores of Palestine and are set adrift. Joseph of Arimathea would be skilled in the art of sailing a boat and, though he would find it difficult without a sure method of propulsion, he would be able to navigate so as to ensure the safety of the other refugees.

The party would not forget that Jesus had charged them to 'Go ye into all the world and PREACH THE GOSPEL' and that would be their aim and that they did in the Marseilles area.

For Joseph of Arimathea, Mary's guardian, though, there would be a much more specific aim, that of getting the most precious and vulnerable person in the band, the Virgin Mary, to the safety of the place Jesus had prepared for her just a couple of years before. He would want to take Mary to the people Jesus had known while he lived in England.

THE JOSEPHIAN MISSION

The days at sea go slowly by and that is where the one tradition leaves them but a separate tradition speaks of the Josephian Mission arriving at Marseilles with the Virgin Mary as one of it's members in the year A.D. 36.

It is one of the great strengths of the traditions that they are unrelated and come of different nations. Yet they interlock rather better than the train connections on a railway timetable.

Another tradition tells the same story from the British point of view and refers to the coming to Glastonbury of the Virgin Mary, Joseph of Arimathea and the Bethany sisters. One of the great hallmarks of the integrity of the traditions is the matter-of-fact way they are written. The writers seem not to have been at all surprised by the fact that the Virgin Mary was at Glastonbury, writing with no more surprise or excitement than we would show by saying the Queen was in London.

From Marseilles we read of the Josephian band travelling across France and following the sea-route Joseph would have taken when he came to England in the course of his business. Joseph would sail around the coast, perhaps calling in on his tin mines in Cornwall, then head up the Bristol Channel, into the mouth of Severn River in sight of the Flat Holme and Steep Holme Islands with the South Wales coast to his left.

At that time Glastonbury was an island and would be easily accessible from the mouth of the Severn by river. Arriving at Burnham on Sea, the refugees would sail up the River Brue to Glastonbury.

THE 'VENGEANCE' OF THE HOLY THORN

It is said that on arriving at Glastonbury Joseph climbed Wyrrall or Weary All Hill and there thrust his staff into the ground much as we do today when put a flag into the ground to claim land as our own. In the course of time, it is said, the staff blossomed and grew. The story used to be a matter of ridicule among those who considered themselves above believing such things but now we know that it is quite possible for a staff, cut in Palestine and kept damp during a long sea journey to actually grow if it is planted.

One fact is sure, the 'Holy Thorn' still exists in the grounds of the Abbey and it BLOOMS AT CHRISTMAS! Often on old Christmas Day. In olden times the British Royal Family were presented with it's blooms each Christmastime, a tradition which, the author is given to understand, has been revived in recent years.

The original Holy Thorn, of which the present three is a cutting, survived on Weary All Hill where it had been 'planted' by Joseph of Arimathea until it was destroyed by a narrow minded religious bigot. A splinter from the thorn flew into his eye and he died soon after.

At Glastonbury too can be seen the 'Chalice Spring' into which Joseph is said to have put the Cup of the Last Supper. At times the water of the spring turns blood red but, as with the growing of the Holy Thorn, there is not necessarily anything supernatural about that. Alas we must admit it to be nothing more than rust colouration when the water coming into the well is at a certain level.

A testimony to the truth of the traditions is the absence of 'miracles' recounted in them. The human mind when inventing stories about holy people tends towards the credulous and usually miracles abound. In the Glastonbury traditions we are told of the staff being thrust into the ground and growing but there is no implication that that happening was supernatural. Hearers assumed it to be supernatural it is true, until it was shown that it could happen by a natural process. It has been said that the Holy Thorn is Leventine, a species not indigenous to Britain and is, in fact, of the species Crataequs monogyna praecox which grows in the Middle East. Even the most ardent sceptic of the Glastonbury traditions has to be impressed by the authorities who affirm that it is almost certain that SOMEONE from the Middle East planted it!

So we have observed the twelve as they left Palestine, we have seen them arrive in Marseilles, journey through France and arrive in Glastonbury where history records that Joseph of Arimathea received the gift of twelve hides of land from Prince Aviragus.

We KNOW from church history that the Christian Church in Britain was founded, at the latest, within a few years of the resurrection and while Rome was yet Pagan. If Joseph of Arimathea did NOT found it then who DID? If someone else founded it then why should tradition have it that it's founder was Joseph of Arimathea?

Joseph of Arimathea was NOT a prominent man or a famous man as far as the Bible record goes. Why then should the whole of the West of England be steeped in traditions about him if they are not true? Rome has no Joseph of Arimathea life, death and burial tradition, neither has Greece, nor has Palestine. Wales has none, Ireland has none and Scotland has none. Why should Cornwall have a multitude of traditions, why should Somerset have a multitude of such traditions and why has Devon, sandwiched between the two not got a 'Joseph tradition'? There would appear to be only one answer and that is that Glastonbury is the place where it all happened!

THE GREAT FIRE

Until 1184 when the Abbey at Glastonbury caught fire it had a library with one of the finest collections of ecclesiastical and historic works in Britain, works which many of those who have studied the subject think would have put beyond doubt the connection of both the Virgin Mary and Joseph of Arimathea to this country. Unfortunately these important records were all destroyed but fortunately there were people who had seen them, copied some of them, remembered parts from other of the ill-fated works and recorded what they knew for the benefit of future generations.

William of Malmesbury was a monk who the monks of Glastonbury invited to stay at the Abbey, writing about A.D. 1126, he would have had access to the records before they were destroyed. He tells us that twelve 'holy missionaries' led by Joseph of Arimathea came to Britain and preached the Incarnation of Jesus Christ. Malmesbury says that the king gave them for their habitation an island covered with trees and bramble bushes and surrounded by marshes, called Yniswytren (Glastonbury).

Maelgwyn of Avalon tells us that Joseph of Arimathea was buried in the old wattle church of St. Mary. The fact is well attested for the body lay there until 1345 when Edward III, and the Abbott of Glastonbury gave permission for one John Bloom to dig for it.

In 1367 R. de Boston, a monk, recorded 'The bodies of Joseph of Arimathea and his companions were found in Glastonbury'.

The earthly remains of Joseph of Arimathea were placed in a silver casket in the crypt under St. Mary Chapel where Holinshed confirms it was in 1577. John Ray says that he personally saw Joseph of Arimathea's tomb there in 1662.

A wave of misguided Puritan verve swept Glastonbury and, to save the tomb of Joseph of Arimathea suffering desecration it was moved to the churchyard of the parish church.

In 1928 the remains were brought into the church and placed in the north transept of St. Katherine's Chapel. There it was regarded as being the tomb of 'John Allen'. Those who had decided upon the new resting place for the tomb of Joseph of Arimathea were forward looking enough to realise that there were still those who may seek the destruction of the tomb of Jesus' uncle.

Who was John Allen? The initials on the tomb are J.A. (Joseph of Arimathea?). There is a badge of Mercury on the tomb, no official badge would be put on the tomb of the unknown 'John Allen'. We are given to understand that the tomb shows signs of a hasty removal from it's resting place.

We must ask ourselves why the tomb of the unknown John Allen should have been moved at all and why it was moved in such haste as to damage the tomb in the way it obviously has been damaged.

If we believe that Jesus of Nazareth was the only begotten Son of God we must wonder why the first Christian Church was established so far from the 'Promised Land', at Glastonbury, and why, over the years, there has been in the Church, of many nations, a general consensus that this is the holiest ground on earth.

14 The Magnet Of The Isles

We have examined two reasons why the Virgin Mary, Jesus and Joseph of Arimathea would have come to Britain rather than go anywhere else in the then known world.

They have been reasons deduced from a reasonable expectation of human behaviour and response and they owe nothing to any supernatural influence.

However no consideration of where the Virgin Mary might have travelled or how she might have lived can ignore the supernatural, for every claim made on her behalf in the scriptures and everything we know of the Virgin Mary cries out in testimony that her life was divinely ordered and therefore, by definition, supernaturally inspired.

Jesus, it is claimed, was the 'only Begotten Son of God' and the whole biblical record of his life is steeped in the miraculous. We are impelled by the very nature of these two people to ask whether there is some overriding influence, an influence other than that which we find in the ordinary order of cause and effect, an influence other than that of mere convenience and expediency which brought the Virgin Mary and Jesus to these shores.

Undoubtedly the 'natural' reason for the Holy Family coming here, convenience, is a powerful one. As we have said, the Holy Family had comparatively easy access to Britain. Uncle Joseph's ships were already trading between Palestine and Britain and it would be surprising if Joseph did not have friends, acquaintances and perhaps relatives here.

The second reason is equally compelling. Mary, Jesus and Joseph would come here because Britain was a highly civilised land with a religion similar to their own patriarchal religion, the religion of ancient Israel. There existed here a climate of tolerance not to be found anywhere else in the world and a depth of knowledge unsurpassed even in ancient Greece. Here they would be safe from the persecutions which afflicted them in Palestine after the birth of Jesus and during his childhood and later from the persecution which followed his resurrection.

The proposition that the Virgin Mary may have been of Cornish descent may have seemed surprising to some who may have thought the line of David existed only in the Middle East. We saw in our chapter on THE ORIGINS OF THE ENGLISH SPEAKING PEOPLES how the ten 'lost' tribes of Israel, as distinct from the two tribed House of Judah, were taken captive into Assyria and migrated westwards until they came to these islands.

There is therefore nothing at all outlandish or even very surprising about the proposition that the Virgin Mary may have been a descendant of royal forebears who were of the dispersion. The fact is that, if our interpretation of the sequence of the migration of Israel is correct, there were probably more 'sons of David' in the British Isles during the lifetime of the Virgin Mary than there were in Palestine.

The more one studies these things the more one is inclined to agree that there are indeed more things in heaven and earth than our knowledge takes into account.

HAVE NATIONS GOT A 'MIGRATIONARY INSTINCT'?

Why did the tribes of Israel migrate from Palestine to these, climatically uninviting, islands at the 'uttermost part' of the earth? The simple answer would be that they drifted aimlessly until they arrived here, but the migrations would seem to be too purposeful for that.

The migrations did not follow one route, nor were they confined to one era of earth's history. The migrations did not cover just one decade, one half-century or even just one century. There is evidence to suggest that the migration of Israel westward commenced either immediately before or soon after the deliverance of Israel from Egypt. The earliest Israelite immigrants had settled in these islands several thousand years before their brethren were taken captive into Assyria.

The Israelites of the migrations have more the character of a flock of birds obeying an inner urge, an inner programming, than they have of a people desperately fleeing before ferocious waves of national persecution. The tendency of the ten tribes to move westward seems to have been within them even when they dwelt in peace in their own land.

It is not as though the nation of Israel moved from places of danger to places of security in their treck westwards. In fact they often moved from places of persecution and danger to places of greater persecution and danger. Sometimes we can trace their migrations from their homeland when there was no persecution or danger at all. They were not to find peace and security in their wanderings, that was something for which they had to wait until they reached these islands. It could not have been apparent to them that, beyond the deprivations of the long journey westward, there was a new life waiting — a new life which many of them would never experience.

We must wonder how they knew they would find peace in the Isles! What 'silent voice' spoke to them and urged them on?

THE SILENT VOICE

At first the idea that there may be some kind of programming inherent in a nation causing it to migrate at a certain time and in a certain direction may seem a little far-fetched but we must consider that the whole of the animal kingdom behaves at the dictates of an 'inner urge' which is beyond the understanding of the species concerned.

The silent voice of nature 'tells' the homing pigeon how to get home and imparts in every living thing a survival instinct. Every animal mother knows how to deliver it's young and how to look after it's young after the offspring has been delivered. We may say without being too cynical that that is another instinct which, apart from the medics among us, we humans are beginning to lose.

When a bird experiences it's first migration season it may well leave for more conducive climes but in the process it often has to pass through LESS conducive climes and face many hazards to get there. How does it KNOW what awaits it at the end of the journey? We call it the 'migrationary instinct' but, though that gives a name to the phenomenon it does not explain it. What we really mean is that it 'hears' a voice which we cannot explain which impels it to move in a certain direction.

If birds and animals have that instinct then is there any reason why groups of people or nations should not have such an instinct? After all man is the most sophisticated animal of all! More specifically had the nation of Israel that migrationary instinct? If a species of bird can have an impulse which it has obeyed for thousands of years then why should we consider it so far fetched that a nation of human beings should have such an instinct?

HIGHER AND LOWER CRITICS

Of course anything with which we are familiar, whether we really understand it or not, we regard as being 'natural'. To that extent animal migration is a natural phenomenon but may there not be something BEYOND the natural, something with which, because it takes hundreds of years rather than hours, days or months, we are not so familiar and therefore regard as being unnatural, supernatural or just plain impossible?

Israel as a nation, or rather as two nations, never claimed to be a natural phenomenon. From it's inception the claim was that it was a 'chosen' people, a people chosen by none other than Jehovah Himself.

Of course, in these materialistic days, the inclination is to put down the idea of a chosen people as being preposterous and not a little anti-social, but is it so preposterous and as for being anti-social who are we, if there be a God in the Christian mould to question his eternal morality? Are we too lightly discarding the supernormal, if not supernatural, experiences of the prophets of old which they recorded in the words 'And the Lord spake unto . . .?

There would certainly seem to have been a 'magnet' in the isles which attracted the people of Israel unto itself. How was that magnet energised? It seems to the author to be worth investigating whether there is some higher reason why the patriarchal religion spread here so soon and was accepted so readily and why Jesus and Mary came here.

Of course if one does not believe in a supernatural being there is some consistency in not believing in anything other than ordinary cause and effect. The thinking of the atheist or agnostic who does not believe in a god or other supernatural influence is quite consistent when it rejects ANY outside influence in the affairs of men. Perhaps though we may be allowed to express surprise that so many who disbelieve in a god who causes things to happen are willing to accept that walking under a ladder, spilling salt, crossing knives or the positioning of the planets at the time of one's birth can cause things to happen. One cannot surely argue reasonably that there is power in a broken mirror to bring seven years bad luck but that there is no power beyond our ken is capable of ordering the affairs of man.

The position of anyone who professes, however vaguely, to believe in a 'one above' is quite different from that of the atheist or agnostic. Once having accepted that a supreme being exists one cannot then go on to argue that there is not the possibility of that being interfering in the history of men and of nations.

Someone who is a more specific believer, a Christian, is forced by the very source of his faith into an acceptance of the supernatural or, as some prefer to think of it, the supernormal. Can there be anything more unbecoming than the posturing of the 'with it' clergy who seem to spend the greater part of their ministries trying to explain that little the Christian Bible teaches can be taken literally.

We will accept for the sake of our investigation the proposition that God chose a nation and ordered it's destiny. It is a hypothesis we can discard easily enough if there is insufficient evidence. In defence of the proposition I would say that it is no more difficult to believe than any other of the foundation beliefs of the Christian Faith.

Though there are apologists who would argue otherwise, I think it is obvious to the unbiased, intelligent, thinking person that the Bible DOES teach that a 'Divine voice' spoke to the prophets of old, that miracles ARE said to have followed the nation of Israel every step of the way from the inception of the nation to the time they disappear from the Bible narrative, that there WAS a Virgin Birth, a miracle strewn life and a resurrection of Jesus Christ. Some will not believe these things actually happened but most people will agree that the Bible TEACHES that they happened.

THE ANCIENT SEERS

Many thousands of years ago there lived in the land of ancient Israel, seers, prophets, men who claimed to be able to foretell the future, especially in respect of the nation of Israel. (Further reading 'The Invisible Hand', published by Megiddo Press).

They believed and proclaimed that earth's history was ordered not by the whims of man but by the will of a 'supreme being' who ordered events according to his will. They claimed to have a unique relationship with their God, they claimed they were able to speak to Him and that He spoke to them.

These prophets not only proclaimed that God chose Israel to be His servant nation but transmitted the laws of the nation, through the prophets, to the people. Their God, they proclaimed, ordered their destiny, their past, their present and their future. He decided where the nation would exist, ordered it's punishments, ordained it's blessings and was the guarantor of it's everlasting existence.

Even in the darkest days when the nation of Israel was ravaged by schism and surrounded by it's enemies, the prophets were looking forward to a glorious future for the whole of the nation of Israel. When the whole nation of Israel dwelt safely in it's own land the prophets made themselves unpopular by fortelling that the House of Judah was to be taken captive, reinstated in their own land and, soon after the Messiah came were to be 'taken captive into all nations'. Their fertile and prosperous land which had flowed 'with milk and honey' was to become a desert, their places of worship were to be desecrated and the Jews find no rest in any nation into which they went. They were not popular prognostications but any student of Jewish history knows that the predictions of the prophets regarding the House of Judah came to pass in detail and to the letter.

The two tribed House of Judah (the Jews) were to be re-established in their own land of Palestine at, what the prophets called, the end of the age. The land was to become fertile again and food would be grown in such abundance that they would be able to export it, they would possess once again the 'high places' of their faith, they would once again worship their God in their land as they had of old, their sons would 'come from afar' and take up residence in their ancient land. Quite obviously those prophecies have come to pass and the Jews are now settled once more in their own land.

The prophets had a very different message for the ten tribes House of

Israel. Though they were to be exiled from their homeland, they were to be given a new land. The ten tribed House of Israel, it was foretold, were to lose their identity, change their language, dwell in a location other than Palestine, become a multitudinous nation and company of nations, and dwell in a safe place.

There can be no doubt in the mind of the discerning reader that not only were the two nations, the House of Israel and the House of Judah, different nations but the propnostications of the prophets reveal their destiny was to be different.

BIBLE PROPHECY THE TEST OF BIBLE INSPIRATION

The story of how the predictions of the prophets were quite literally fulfilled is one of the most cogent arguments for the Divine Inspiration of the Bible there is. It is, too, an argument which Jesus used to great effect on the road to Emmaus. We are told that 'Beginning at Moses and ALL the prophets, he expounded unto them, in ALL the scriptures, the things concerning himself.' (Luke 24:17) That great preacher Principal George Jeffreys used to say 'Bible prophecy is the test of Bible inspiration' and he was right! For those who wish to follow my arguments more closely I give references as to where they can be found in the Bible.

The sceptre and the books of the law were to remain with the House of Judah and Judah (the Jews) were to remain in Jerusalem until the Messiah came. That was quite literally fulfilled for, though the House of Israel went captive into Assyria never to return, the House of Judah always had a presence in Palestine and were in the land at the time of the coming of Jesus the Messiah. The corollary of saying 'The sceptre shall not depart from Judah nor the lawgiver from between his feet until Shiloh (the Messiah) come' is that when 'Shiloh' DID come then the sceptre WOULD depart from Judah.

Not long after the time of Jesus even the tenuous kingships of the Herods disappeared and there has been no king of Judah on earth from that time.

Jesus himself warned Judah that the Kingdom was to be taken from them when he said 'The kingdom of God shall be taken from you, and given to a nation bringing forth the fruits of it.' (Matthew 21:43).

Is it by chance that within months of his pronouncement the kingship of Judah began to slip from the grasp of the Herods? Is it a further coincidence that at the precise time it was slipping from the grasp of the Herods, in these British islands there was growing a tradition of Christian monarchy which has not been extinguished to this day?

In view of the promise made by Jacob to Judah thousands of years before the time of Christ is it mere coincidence that Judah LOST the kingship when Shiloh came and that at the 'uttermost part of the earth' another nation began to nurture the faith in it's royal family? It is a matter of history but is it also coincidental that at the time predicted by the ancient seer that it would happen the centre of 'Shiloh's' faith shifted from Jerusalem to Glastonbury?

THE PRIME 'FRUIT'

We may well listen to the words of Jesus again 'The kingdom of God shall be taken from you (the Jews), and given to a nation bringing forth the fruits thereof.' The one 'fruit' of which he would be speaking would be his gospel for, whatever WE may think of it, there can be no doubt that there was nothing Jesus regarded more highly than the preaching of the gospel.

If we can find which group of nations have been responsible, more than any other, for the propagation of the gospel of Jesus Christ then it follows that we have found the nation to whom 'the kingdom of God' was to be given. Find the nation who brought forth the 'fruits' Jesus expected and we have found to which nation he transferred the kingdom.

As we have seen, the nation which carried the banner of the gospel of Jesus Christ when Christianity was being persecuted and rejected in Palestine and rejected throughout the whole civilised and pagan world, was none other than the British nation.

Later in history, and there are few who would gainsay the fact, the British Empire and the United States of America, followed closely by the Scandinavian nations, were the prime movers in the evangelisation of the world. Of course, nations are never perfect, ancient Israel certainly was not, but if we take an overall view of the history of the English speaking peoples we have to agree that no other nations on earth have brought forth what we would consider to be the 'fruits' of the Christian message more clearly than this race.

The British, American and Scandinavian nations have their detractors but I believe that actions speak louder than words and, whatever people may say about us, to whom do they turn when oppression threatens? One cannot imagine that if our past is as bad as it has been painted so many people of different colours, faiths and cultures would have chosen Britain and American as their home.

There is a famous cartoon which appeared in the First World War. Two soldiers are seen standing up to their waists in water in a shellhole. The surrounding area is a cratered desolation. One soldier is complaining about his lot and receives the reply 'Look Bill if you can find a better 'ole go to it!'

Seemingly very few people who complain about life in Britain and America can find a 'better ole'!

It would appear that the ordinary people of the nations we have ruled have a different view of Britain and America from the electioneering views of some of our politicians.

The Soviet Union has no immigration problem, they have to build walls to keep people IN! Which communist country DOES have an immigration problem? Which nations on earth are the nations to which people want to immigrate? The English speaking nations! Based upon my belief that people themselves know best what is good for them I would suggest that much of the constant denigration of Britain and America is Soviet inspired political sniping.

When Jesus spoke the words to which I have referred Rome was pagan, Greece was a halfway house between agnosticism and superstition, religion in the Holy Land had fallen into the hands of the Pharisees and Sadducees. The only nation at that time which could be said to be bringing forth the 'fruits' of which Jesus spoke was Britain.

THE PROPHETS AND ISRAEL'S FUTURE

Nothing which happened to the ten tribed House of Israel had not been predicted before it happened. If you read the Old Testament you will see that all that happened to both the House of Judah and the House of Israel was predicted many hundreds, sometimes thousands, of years before the event.

Having floated the hypothesis that the British, American, Celtic, Anglo-Saxon and Scandinavian peoples are the descendants of the House of Israel we would expect to find the history of, what we shall call for convenience 'the English speaking people', to compare with the predictions of the ancient seers regarding the, then, future of the ten tribes.

There are very definite and clear prophetic statements as to:

1. The 'size' of the House of Israel in it's new habitations.
2. The place to which they would go and the way in which they would then spread.
3. The period of history in which they would emerge from obscurity and take the centre of the world stage.

THE HOUSE OF ISRAEL WAS TO BECOME A 'GREAT' AND MIGHTY NATION'

Keep in mind the 'line of promise' as we have previously traced it and think of the following prediction about the House of Israel made 1450 years before Jesus was born.

> 'And I will make thee a great nation, and I will bless thee, and MAKE THY NAME GREAT; and thou shalt be a blessing. And I will bless them that bless thee and curse them that curse thee.'
> Genesis 12:2.

'I will make thy name GREAT'. It is certainly no proof of our Israelitish identity but nevertheless it is of interest that this nation became known as GREAT BRITAIN. No-one, I think, will deny that the English speaking peoples fulfill that prophecy spoken 3400 years ago.

THE HOUSE OF ISRAEL WAS TO BECOME 'A NATION AND COMPANY OF NATIONS'

> 'And God said unto him (Jacob), Thy name is Jacob: thy name shall not be called any more Jacob, but Israel shall be thy name: and he called his name Israel. And God said unto him, I am God Almighty: be fruitful and multiply; A NATION AND COMPANY OF NATIONS shall be of thee, and kings shall come out of thy loins.' Genesis 35: 10, 11, 12

Britain DID indeed become a 'company of nations'. Not only is there the Commonwealth of Nations but also the United States of America sprang from the same stock. There has never been an organisation of nations on earth at all like the United States of America and the British Commonwealth of Nations. There is the so called Union of Soviet Socialist Republics, but that is held together by the tyranny of oppression not the free-will of it's people and states.

The member states of the United States of America are member states from choice NOT conquest and the members of the British Commonwealth of Nations remain in the Commonwealth because they believe in it not because they are coerced.

Let me remind those who would say that the Arab nations also descended from Abraham that the line of promise did NOT pass through the father of the Arab nations, nor through Judah, the father of the Jewish nation but through Ephraim and Manasseh. The promise could not have, nor has it, been fulfilled in the Arabs or the Jews — it was not intended to be. Both those peoples have a different and honourable destiny.

AFTER LEAVING THE PROMISED LAND — IN WHAT KIND OF PLACE WERE THE TEN TRIBES OF THE HOUSE OF ISRAEL TO SETTLE?

We have seen that Palestine was to be the permanent home of the Jews. Though they were to be scattered among the nations they were never to lose their identity and they were always assured of their return to Palestine at the 'end of the age'. There was never a time in history when the Jews were 'lost', they kept their religion, much of their language and their links with Palestine.

The destiny of the House of Israel was to be quite different. Samuel records:

> 'Moreover I (God Almighty) will appoint a place for my people Israel, and will plant them, that they may dwell in a place of their own, AND MOVE NO MORE . . .' 2. Samuel 7:10

That place could NOT have been Palestine because God had appointed that place for Israel many years before and they already possessed it at the time Samuel wrote those words. Sensible interpretation demands that the 'appointed place' referred to by Samuel was a place OTHER than Palestine.

Once settled in the 'appointed place' they were to 'move no more'. That cannot be said of the Jews in Palestine whose whole history has been one of movement in and out of captivity. Once the tribes had arrived in Britain they did NOT move again.

Over a thousand years after Samuel had written, John the Divine wrote on the same subject while he was on the Isle of Patmos. He wrote a prophecy of a 'woman clothed with the sun, and the moon under her feet, and upon her head a crown of twelve stars'. The reference is, of course, the nation of Israel. John saw 'a great red dragon' persecute the woman and wrote:

> 'The woman fled into the wilderness, where she hath a place prepared of God, that they should feed her there a thousand two hundred and three score days.' Revelation 12:6

The 'appointed place' and the 'place prepared of God' are, from the context, seen to be one and the same place. Both Samuel and John contend that Israel's migration to the British Isles was no chance happening but part of a 'Divine plan'. Certainly, as we have seen, the westward movement of the tribes of Israel was too persistent and too purposeful to have been anything other than an 'inspired' migration, whether we accept that as being in the sense that the migration of a bird is inspired or look to a higher form of inspiration.

The scenario for the House of Israel was to be that danger would threaten and they would move to a place, other than Palestine, which was a second 'Promised Land'. Once there they would never move again.

Jeremiah, the weeping prophet, writing after the House of Israel had been taken captive into Assyria, describes the new promised land with more detail when he writes:

> 'At the same time, saith the Lord, will I be God of all the families of Israel, and they shall be MY people. Thus saith the Lord, THE PEOPLE WHICH WERE LEFT OF THE SWORD FOUND GRACE IN THE WILDERNESS.' Jeremiah 31:1,2

It is the word 'wilderness' which has hidden from so many commentators the truth. In their search for their ten lost tribes they have concentrated on small bands of primitive people living in infertile and out-of-the-way places. They have missed entirely the point that the ten tribes of Israel were to be a nation whose name was called 'great', a 'nation and company of nations' and have concentrated on the one word 'wilderness'.

The word, in fact, had no connotations that the land to which Israel were to go was to be a desert or wasteland. The word translated 'wilderness' is, in the original, 'midbar' and Young's Analytical Concordance translates it 'Wilderness, desert, pasture land'.

That it should be interpreted 'Pasture land' in this instance is to be seen from Isaiah's prophecy on the same subject:

> 'Sing unto the Lord a new song, and HIS praise from the END OF THE EARTH, ye that go down to the sea, and all that is therein: THE ISLANDS, and the inhabitants thereof. Let the WILDERNESS and the cities thereof lift up their voice, the villages that Kedar doth inhabit: let the inhabitants of the rock sing, let them shout from the top of the mountains. Let them give glory unto the Lord, and declare his praise IN THE ISLANDS.'

The important points to note in that prophecy are:

1. The 'wilderness' was NOT a place of bareness and sadness but a place of plenty and gladness.

2. The 'wilderness' or 'pasture land' in which the House of Israel was to dwell was to be situated in the Isles.

3. The 'Isles' were to be situated at 'the end of the earth' from Palestine.

That at once rules out any barren place and any place near to Palestine as being the new home of the House of Israel.

The 'end of the earth' as it was known in Isaiah's time was the North Sea coast of Europe and the Isles which were at the uttermost part of the earth were none other than the British Isles.

Jeremiah the prophet, speaking of the Isles in which Israel were dwelling describes them as being '. . . the isles which ARE AFAR OFF . . .' (Jeremiah 31:10).

Some students, who should know better, have identified the Isles in which the ten tribes were to settle as being one or more of the islands in the Mediterranean. Quite apart from the fact that none of the Mediterranean islands is capable of supporting a 'great and mighty nation' nor a people whose population was, as the prophet foretold, multitudinous as the sand of the sea. Nor can the Mediterranean islands be said to be 'afar off' from Palestine nor at the 'END OF THE EARTH'.

THE 'END OF THE EARTH' NORTH-WEST OF PALESTINE

We should note the precise words used by the prophet, the Isles in which Israel was to dwell were to be 'at the END of the earth' not as is so often misquoted at the 'ENDS' of the earth.

So we have seen that The House of Israel was to be banished from Palestine, was to lose it's name Israel and be called by a name which would be thought of as 'great', would leave it's old religion and find a new religion, would lose it's language and speak a new language, would occupy a 'pasture land' which was to be in islands 'afar off' from Palestine and situated at 'the end of the earth' from Palestine. That nation was to bring forth the 'fruits' of the message of the Messiah of Israel when he came. Now I ask you, does all that not almost certainly identify the BRITISH ISLES?

Could not the uttermost part of the earth have been in a different direction? Where in a different direction is there a nation which had a Christian Church before any other nation on earth? The prophet Isaiah (49:12) speaks of the children of Israel as coming 'from afar' from the 'north and from the west', which is the Hebrew way of saying the north-west. So the isles of which the prophets had spoken were to the north-west of Palestine. THE BRITISH ISLES ARE SITUATED AT THE, AS WAS

THEN THOUGHT, 'END OF THE EARTH' TO THE NORTH-WEST OF PALESTINE!

That is not all that the prophets foretold about the future of the House of Israel after they had settled in the Islands. They were to expand territorially, they were to inherit a Gentile empire and they were to develop desolate parts of the earth (Isaiah 54: 1-3).

The inhabitants of the British Islands did just that. Quite suddenly, no-one can really understand what motivated them, the inhabitants of these islands began to 'enlarge the place of their tent'. The British people DID inherit many Gentile countries and populate many desolate areas, among them Canada, Australia, New Zealand, Newfoundland and, through the Pilgrim Fathers, the United States of America.

Inexplicably, almost one might say, miraculously, from this little island seemingly asleep in the dank mists of the Atlantic, colonisers poured forth and established a worldwide population of English speaking peoples. Wildernesses began to flourish where there had been desolation before, civilisations were established where before there had been the multitudinous cruelties of tribalism, cities were built which later other peoples were to be proud to possess and a way of life was propogated which became the envy of the world.

Quite literally Britain fulfilled the three predictions Isaiah made for the future of the House of Israel (1) Spreading abroad from their Island home. (2) Inheriting Gentile nations and (3) Bringing desolate places under development. It would seem that if the British are NOT the descendants of Ten Tribed Israel then they are fulfilling ALL the promises and predictions made by the ancient prophets to that nation!

There is yet another prediciton which we find in Genesis 28:14 regarding HOW Israel would spread 'And thy seed shall be as the dust of the earth, and thou shalt spread abroad to the WEST, and to the EAST, and to the NORTH, and to the SOUTH:'

Had the prophet said North, south, east and west, that would have been the order in which we generally mention the points of the compass but he did not. The prophet said west, east, north and south — why? Is it pure chance that that is the exact sequence in which the colonisation from these islands took place? To Newfoundland to the WEST, then to India in the EAST, then to Canada in the NORTH and South Africa in the SOUTH. Could it be that the prophet was foretelling British history many thousands of years before it happened?

There is no doubt in the minds of many authorities who have no 'axe to grind' that among the first people who inhabited this land were people who originated somewhere in the area of the River Euphrates. That much, many regard as a matter of fact. We have discussed the strong probability that migrants from ancient Israel moved westwards and settled in these islands.

All that we ascertained from an examination of purely secular happenings and evidence.

In this chapter however, we have come to see that there were predictions, spoken very early on in the history of the nation of Israel, which foretold where the House of Israel was to dwell, what kind of people they would be when they dwelt there and what would happen to them. We have examined the possibility that those predictions were fulfilled in the British Islands.

It is one thing to say that a nation has moved from one place to another and quite another to suggest that, that they should do so had been foretold many thousands of years before it happened. The first proposition is temporal but the second much more important. We are now suggesting that the migrations of Israel were a form of Divine predestination, of Divine instigation. Such an assumption leads us not only to a different view of history but to a new view of life. No longer do we see mankind plunging hither and thither out of control but we see a guiding hand in the affairs of mankind.

If Jesus was the long awaited Messiah of Israel, not only of the Jews but of the WHOLE nation of Israel, then is it not to be expected that he would visit the majority of his people where the majority of his people were living? Is it so surprising that the mother of Jesus should have visited the cities of the ten tribes just as she visited the cities of the two tribes?

No! That is not altogether the question, the question must be whether it is not unreasonable and ridiculous even to believe that, under those circumstances, Jesus and Mary DID NOT visit these islands.

15 Did The Virgin Mary Live and Die in England?

The time has come to bring all the 'loose ends' together!

Throughout our investigation we have been faced with alternatives and we have had to ask ourselves which of those alternatives, in the circumstances of the time, were the most likely to have happened.

We must 'get into' the reality of the years immediately following the birth of Jesus and try to relive the excitement, expectation and even disbelief his birth would have engendered.

If we accept that Jesus was indeed born of a virgin as the Bible tells us; that the Astrologers of both Babylon and Jerusalem had been predicting the conjuction of the three stars for years; that the 'star' of Bethlehem actually appeared; that the manger WAS visited by wise men, Magi or Astrologers from the East; that herald angels DID exhort the shepherds when Jesus was born, and, that Herod DID conduct a 'slaughter of the innocents' out of fear of the new born King, then the various questions we have asked simply DEMAND an answer.

Is it reasonable to accept that, if they had remained in Palestine, this unique conception, surrounded by such unusual events would have been so soon forgotten that Jesus and his mother could have lived there without publicity or comment for some thirty-eight years? Is it reasonable to believe that the whole of the life of Jesus and Mary would have been completely ignored if they had been in Palestine? Would not the early life of the miraculous mother and child have been the inspiration for constant speculation and writing? Why, apart from the passover incident when Jesus was twelve, is there no record of anything he said or did?

Why do we read nothing about Jesus, apart from the passover incident, until he was about forty? Why do we read nothing about Mary until Jesus was about forty?

Some will say because he did not declare himself to be Messiah until then but we have seen that to be a strange theory indeed! Did not the Star of Bethlehem, the Wise Men and the Herald Angels proclaim him to be the Messiah at his birth? Did not Mary herself make that very proclamation in the 'Magnificat' and did not Simeon declare that Jesus was the Messiah in the beautiful song of Simeon?

If we want an unbiased assessment of the events of that first Christmas does not Herod, albeit unwittingly, give us that witness?

Did not Herod HIMSELF, having studied the astrological predictions and the prophetic predictions, tell us by his actions that, in his opinion, Jesus was none other than the Messiah of Israel, born that day in Bethlehem? Did he not proclaim the fact, that his comprehension of the ancient prophecies, a comprehension which seemed not to have been shared by the religious leaders of his day, was that they were being fulfilled in Jesus?

No ordinary and unsubstantiated claim of a young girl that her conception was of God would have been so alarming to him that he would have unleashed the slaughter of the innocents! Was it not Herod's understanding, the understanding of the Wise Men, the understanding of the Shepherds that this child was THE MESSIAH, THE KING OF THE JEWS?

Yet, we are asked to believe, this furore was forgotten and Jesus lived for thirty-eight years without comment from those who had been there on that miraculous nativity day!

Why, if Jesus was 'saving himself' for later years did he go out of his way at the age of twelve to demonstrate that he should be about his Father's business? He was obviously preaching and debating then! Did he suddenly stop being about his Father's business when he was twelve and not start again until he was forty. Why should he do that?

Are we to imagine, and does it hold credence if we do imagine it, that Jesus did not preach or debate his message in the whole of his life except on that one occasion at the Passover when he was twelve? Can we believe that after that one statement he stayed silent until he was forty or so years of age?

If he did not remain silent during those years then one would not expect him to have preached any other message than the one for which the religious hierarchy so savagely attacked him when he was forty years of age. Then why did they not attack him sooner, if he had been saying the same thing for thirty years or so? Why did their hatred burst forth so much later and why was it then that they started to interrogate him, at a time so late in his ministry when the damage was almost done?

Jesus seemed not to have had any disciples or followers in Palestine prior to that fateful last year of his life. Again we must ask — why? Would it not be more natural, in view of the astonishing events at his birth, that he would have gathered around himself people who agreed with him, or were at the least curious, much sooner?

We have questioned why there is no record, not only in the New Testament but in any other contemporary manuscript, of the family life of

Jesus. We THINK of him, and there have been many imaginative sermons about him, being brought up in his father's carpenter's shop in Nazareth but there is no record of him having been an apprentice carpenter in the Bible! We owe that flight of imagination to preachers and bible commentators who seem hard pressed to explain the thirty-eight year silence.

There is no mention to be found of the kind of relationship he had with his foster father Joseph or of the activities of the Virgin Mary in Palestine.

No one who is REALLY interested in the story of Jesus and his mother Mary can put such questions into 'limbo', they are questions which DEMAND answers. The whole silence does not correspond with what we know of human nature.

THE MYSTERY WOMAN OF THE APOCALYPSE

Yet, though, tradition is silent in the land of Jesus' birth there is no such silence in British tradition. We have seen that traditions regarding Jesus' presence in Cornwall and Somerset during his childhood abound. It is evident that Joseph of Arimathea was in the tin trade and we must be impressed by the fact that the traditions concentrate on Somerset and Cornwall. Where there is, or has been, no tin neither is there a tradition! We see from this that the traditions regarding Jesus' coming to Britain are not at all indiscriminate, there is a definite link with the tin trade.

Every circumstance cries out that Jesus was NOT in Palestine during those silent years and, in view of the early death of her husband Joseph, all reason cries out that Mary was not there either. Again our knowledge of human nature tells us that wherever Jesus went Mary would go too. If the Gospel narratives are true and Mary undoubtedly KNEW what a precious child she had borne then would she have lightly let him travel so far for so long without having visited him?

'But' someone will say 'why has it not been more plainly said in tradition that the Virgin Mary came to Britain if it is true?'

We have noted that the Virgin Mary would, like her son, have many enemies. We have seen too that, even in those days, the long arm of terror was international. It would have made good sense for her enemies to have been precluded from a knowledge of where she was and for her friends not to say where she was. The point though is that, if she had been in Palestine, EVERYONE would have known where she was!

There is a scripture which is taken as referring to the nation of Israel and we believe it does, but it could also be a veiled indication to the faithful of what had happened to the Virgin Mary. John the Divine, writing in A.D. 95 said:

'And there appeared a great wonder in heaven — a WOMAN clothed with the sun, and the moon under her feet, and upon her head a crown of twelve stars.
And she, being with child, cried, travailing in birth, and pained to be delivered.
And there appeared another wonder in heaven; and, behold, a great red dragon, having seven heads and ten horns, and seven crowns upon his heads.
And his tail drew the third part of the stars of heaven and did cast them to the earth; and the dragon stood before the woman who was ready to be delivered, to devour her child as soon as it was born.
SHE BROUGHT FORTH A MALE CHILD, who was to rule all nations with a rod of iron; and her child was CAUGHT UP UNTO GOD, and to his throne.
AND THE WOMAN FLED INTO THE WILDERNESS, WHERE SHE HATH A PLACE PREPARED BY GOD . . .'

Revelation 12:1-6

All the elements of the Virgin Mary story are there.

The Red Dragon was at that time a symbol of the Pagan Roman Empire (see the author's book THE INVISIBLE HAND, published by Megiddo Press). The Virgin Mary was indeed chosen by God as the representative of the whole nation of Israel, hence the twelve stars.

An enemy WAS there at the birth of Jesus prepared to devour the child — the massacre of the innocents by Herod.

Her child WAS caught up to his Father's throne — the ascension.

The Virgin Mary DID flee into the wilderness. As we have seen the prophets spoke of the British Isles, the place to which the House of Israel was to migrate as 'the wilderness'.

Bible students are not unfamiliar with the fact that prophecies often have both a prime and secondary meaning. We may wonder if this is a prophecy which has a prime and secondary meaning.

Does the 'crown' this woman is seen to be wearing have something to do with her being of royal blood? Certainly there are respects in which that statement of John's could more aptly refer to the Virgin Mary than to the nation of Israel.

The prophecy of John, and I use the word 'prophecy' in it's widest meaning, would in fact fit her life precisely if she was the 'Marcella' who was in the oarless boat which was set adrift on the Mediterranean soon after Jesus was 'caught up unto God, and to his throne.' She would quite literally have 'fled into the wilderness'.

THE EFFECT OF OUR PROPOSITION ON THE CHRISTIAN GOSPEL

How does that interpretation of the passage in Revelation affect the fundamentalist Christian faith? How indeed does our proposition that the Virgin Mary lived many years of her life, died and was buried in England affect Christian teaching?

The answer is not at all from the point of view of Christian theology. The doctrines of the Virgin Birth, the sinless life, the atoning death, the resurrection and the Deity of Jesus remain unaffected.

After all, the Virgin Mary HAD to live and die somewhere and it is difficult to see how the speculation that she did so in England rather than Palestine detracts from the Christian gospel at all.

There ARE positive factors however. The unique part the English speaking peoples have played in the propagation of the gospel is both emphasised and explained by our thesis.

Some have argued that because Jesus was apparently unknown at the time of the commencement of his ministry the miraculous events of the first Christmas could not have happened. It has been a real stumbling block for many critics that someone whose birth was said to be surrounded by so much that was extraordinary should have been 'forgotten' so soon and until quite late in life. They are of course right to suggest that such miraculous happenings would not be so easily forgotten in a land in which quite unimportant events were elevated to traditions. Who forgot Samson having his hair cut? Who forgot Goliath being killed by a pebble?

The proposition that Mary and Jesus spent a considerable time in Britain adds veracity to the Bible story, changing our view of the events of that first Christmas from being that of a myth to a reality. Viewing the Virgin Mary and Jesus in a real world-wide context, it is much easier to believe that God DID indeed manifest Himself in the flesh. It would be difficult to see why the God of the Universe should come to the House of Judah and ignore the, from the point of view of the promises to the Patriarchs, more important House of Israel.

We find ourselves no longer having to grapple with the inexplicable silence which has worried Bible commentators for so long.

There is another important point about the tracing of Israel to these Islands, to the Commonwealth and to the United States of America which fundamentalists might wish to consider. It is that without there being a House of Israel, as well as a Jewish State of Israel (House of Judah) on earth today, their God can be shown to have failed in His promises to that nation.

Fundamentalist Christianity depends for it's dogma upon the teaching that God NEVER fails and God NEVER changes His mind. Fundamentalists must come to terms with the fact that God gave promises not only to the House of Judah but to the House of Israel. If He has not fulfilled those promises to the House of Israel but, as some would contend, decided to fulfil them in some other institution — the church — then I can only hope that He behaves rather better toward the Fundamentalist Church. Otherwise they may find that, in the course of time, He has taken the promise of salvation which He has given to them, and which they rightly hold so dear, and transferred it to someone else!

A very perceptive Jew writing in the Jewish Chronicle as early as 1879 said:

> 'the Scriptures speak of the future restoration, of Israel, which is clearly to include both Judah and Ephraim. The problem then is reduced to it's simplest form. THE TEN TRIBES ARE CERTAINLY IN EXISTENCE. All that has to be done is to discover which people represent them.'
>
> The Jewish Encyclopaedia wrote:
>
> 'If the Ten Tribes have disappeared, the literal fulfilment of the prophecies would be impossible. If they have not disappeared obviously they must exist under a different name.'

Surely nobody who is interested in proving the inspiration of the Bible, as the fundamentalists are, can be indifferent to the existence of the Ten Tribes of Israel.

THE DOCTRINE OF THE BODILY ASSUMPTION OF THE VIRGIN MARY

It will be seen that much of our evidence for the coming to this country of Joseph of Arimathea and the antiquity of the British Church comes from ancient Catholic sources. It will too be seen, by the language they use, that the evidence we will produce for the interment of the Virgin Mary at Glastonbury comes from those who are of the Catholic tradition. The evidence is the stronger for that, for the ancient Catholic clerics had no reason to aggrandise these Islands and we are not interested here in doctrine but in history. Vatican history is probably as reliable as anyone elses.

What then of the modern Roman Catholic doctrine that the Virgin Mary did NOT die but ascended into heaven in the same manner that Christ ascended into heaven?

The doctrine of the bodily assumption of the Virgin Mary was not adopted by the Roman Catholic Church until fairly recently. Until then pilgrims to Jerusalem were shown the Chapel of Dormiton, the place, even the very ledge where the Virgin Mary was said to have died. There are still many Roman Catholic theologians who do not accept the doctrine of the bodily ascension of the Virgin Mary. It is difficult to see why such an important event as the bodily assumption of the Virgin Mary would not have become dogma sooner had there been any evidence for it.

The bodily assumption was NOT what the ancient Catholic clerics taught, as we shall see.

DIRECT EVIDENCE FOR THE LIFE, DEATH AND BURIAL OF THE VIRGIN MARY IN ENGLAND

The ENCYCLOPAEDIA BRITANNICA says of William of Malmesbury that he was 'the foremost historian of his time.' He was educated at Malmesbury Abbey and studied logic, physics, moral philosophy and history.

Born in A.D. 1090 he would have access to the important library of Glastonbury Abbey before it was destroyed by fire. In fact Malmesbury was specially commissioned by the Abbot of Glastonbury to write the history of the church from it's foundation and was given a unique access to the library. He produced the authorative De Antiquitate Glastoniae.

In his ACTS OF THE KINGS OF THE ENGLISH Malmesbury writes of Glastonbury Abbey, and, after telling how the church was respected from the earliest times, goes on to say that it is the 'depository of so many saints'. He concludes 'who there especially chose to await the day of resurrection under the protection of THE MOTHER OF GOD.'

That can mean nothing other than that the Virgin Mary was buried there. If he was speaking of the immortal soul of the Virgin Mary then the saints could have been buried ANYWHERE and have awaited 'the day of the resurrection under the protection of the Mother of God'.

For centuries the rich and famous, kings and princes and saints of the church sought to be buried in Glastonbury 'under the protection of the Mother of God.' It was not until AFTER the great fire at the Abbey that the details of the Virgin Mary's life and death at Glastonbury became obscured.

On the wall of the Lady Chapel there were two names which, for hundreds of years, puzzled those who studied the Abbey at Glastonbury. It is a very old inscription 'Jesus - Maria'. Authorities consider that it is a very ancient stone recovered from the original stone church.

A very cogent argument FOR the life, death and burial of the Virgin Mary at Glastonbury is put forward by Rev. Lionel Smithett Lewis, one time Vicar of Glastonbury (St. Joseph of Arimathea at Glastonbury, published by James Clarke and Company). He makes the point that church dedications to the Virgin Mary did not begin before the year A.D. 1130, except that is, for St. Mary's, Glastonbury. Prior to that, he intimates, churches had been dedicated to the Trinity, St. Michael or SOMEONE WHO WAS BURIED THERE. Was St. Mary's, Glastonbury an exception or was IT named after the Virgin Mary BECAUSE SHE WAS BURIED THERE?

I have put forward the idea that the Virgin Mary might have been put aboard one of his boats travelling to England by Joseph of Arimathea. We know that there were twelve people in the boat which was set adrift during the persecution and that corresponds to the 'twelve hides of land' given to the 'boat people' when they arrived here, a fact attested to in the Domesday Book.

There is an ancient and authoritative writing of Maelgwyn, who wrote about A.D. 540 which tells of the burial place of Joseph of Arimathea adjacent to St. Mary's Chapel in Glastonbury. The Reverend Lewis, translating this ancient writing, has Maelgwyn describe Joseph's grave thus:

> 'Next to the south corner of the house of prayer, made of prepared wattles OVER the adorable powerful Virgin by the aforesaid circles of THIRTEEN inhabiting that place.'

So we DO have a very ancient, authoritative and direct statement that not only Joseph of Arimathea but also the Virgin Mary are buried at Glastonbury.

I have mentioned before the fact that John Leland, who held Henry VIII's licence to search for ancient records in the abbeys of Britain tells how, in A.D. 1534, he examined Maelgwyn of Avalon's Historia de Rebus Britannicis in the Glastonbury Abbey Library and found the following:

> The Isle of Avalon 'received thousands of sleepers, among them Joseph de Marmore from Arimathea by name, entered his perpetual sleep. And he lies in a bifurcated line next the southern angle of the oratory made of circular wattles by 13 inhabitants of the place OVER THE ADORABLE AND POWERFUL VIRGIN.'

THE END OF THE TRAIL OF DISCOVERY?

I think not! Because historians have accepted so easily and with surprising acquiescence Rome's less than authoritive view of the British, research into the history of Britain in the late B.C. and early A.D. years has not been extensive or persistent.

Students, unless they are advanced students of history, can be forgiven for thinking that we have no ascertainable history prior to the second coming of the Romans to these shores.

There is yet a lot of evidence to be unearthed by the spade of the archaeologist, evidence which will give a more illuminated view of the times in which our ancestors lived than has hitherto been the case, because of modern technology. There is, too , much research to do into the documents which are already available to historians. Undoubtedly the next few years will bring some startling discoveries about our past and the real identity of those nations which are spoken of as having sprung from the British race.

It may be argued that what happened in those dim and distant B.C. years is of little importance today but to argue that is to debase history and to suggest that the relevance and importance of history resides exclusively in it's practical value.

Even judged by THAT soul-less criterion though, what happened in the progress of the English speaking peoples in the years before and after the birth of Jesus is important. Standing, as they do, in the vanguard of freedom, as the guardians of all that civilised people hold dear, the bulwark against the forces of tyranny, the English speaking peoples have a more noble function today than at any time in their history. They are the ONLY guarantors of freedom, the only people with the strength to withstand the most odious international oppressor of people the world has ever known. It is important that we shake off the dark doubts about ourselves which the Soviet propagandists have so assiduously caused to fester in our minds, it is important that we should comprehend our destiny and adjust our national life to it.

Having said that, it is better NOT to debase history and regard it as a purely utilitarian study. Trafalgar cannot easily be seen to have a contemporary value unless it is to help our young people find their identity and to instill in them and us a sense of pride in our country. Contrary to the views of many people, too many people, patriotism IS an important quality. In the ultimate no one will protect the Briton except the British and no one will protect the American except the American. We have witnessed all too often the decline, fall and then persecution of peoples who have lost their national pride. Whatever our humanistic dreams the stark reality is that internationalism is more easily extended to others than attracted to oneself, there is no substitute, in the long term, for national self-help.

My purpose in writing this book was to throw the question 'DID THE VIRGIN MARY LIVE AND DIE IN ENGLAND?' and all the attendant questions open to discussion rather than to prove a point. Though I personally would come down on the side of acceptance of the traditions that the Virgin Mary DID live and die here, it would be pretentious of me to claim to have proved the point beyond any shadow of a doubt. If such an admission is considered by some to be a fault I can take comfort in the knowledged that very few of even the 'facts' of science have not had to be revised if not abrogated over the years. So many of the things dogmatists will tell us are unassailable truths prove to be far less than that when they stand before the spotlight of new knowledge.

There remains however a reasoned argument albeit an argument based, to some extent, on circumstantial evidence, that the Virgin Mary DID live and die at Glastonbury, England.

We should give full weight to the fact that circumstantial evidence is often more reliable than an eyewitness account of an event. Few murderers would be brought to justice if the law did not give full weight to circumstantial evidence, yet any court would be loath to convict on the uncorroberated evidence of one eye-witness alone.

It is of course a tactic of those who wish not to believe, to stretch the admittedly long arm of coincidence to altogether unbelievable lengths. There is a point in the collection of any evidence at which we, if we are to be considered impartial investigators, abandon the explanation of 'coincidence' in favour of cause and effect.

The migration of birds serves as an illustration. Not ALL birds migrate and not all birds that migrate, migrate to the same place. Yet the migration of birds is a phenomenon too consistent for us to contend that thousands of birds flying to the same place at a certain time of the year is coincidence.

A jury is faced with the evidence that tyre marks which correspond with those of the prisoner's car were found at the site of the murder. Certainly NOT proof of the guilt of the accused — there are probably thousands of tyres with the same tread in that part of the country.

Further evidence, a scraping of paint is produced, it was taken from a gatepost a few feet from where the body was found and is similar to the paint on the accused's car. There is too, a little damage to his car at about the same height from the ground as the point at which the paint scraping was taken from the gatepost. Still not proof but NOW we would be foolish not to admit that there is a case to answer.

A button is produced, which was found at the scene of the crime, and it matches the buttons on a coat belonging to the accused, from which there is a similar button missing. Of course it is true that there will be thousands of similar coats, with the same kind of buttons and there is a probability that a number of those coats will have buttons missing. The button is not in itself, proof.

The killer scratched himself on a bush and some of his blood was found on the victim's body. The accused's blood group matches the group of the blood found on the victim. But there are thousands of people with the same blood group as the accused! The blood found on the victim is NOT IN ITSELF conclusive proof that the accused was the murderer. Though there was a scratch on his arm which was consistent with him having been injured by a thorn from a bush of the kind to be found at the site of the killing, that was not PROOF either because there must be thousands of such bushes on which he could have scratched himself.

Even the fact that the wallet of the victim was found in the pocket of the accused did not prove that the accused had been the killer. There is the remotest of possibilities that the accused found the wallet while walking in a street many miles from the scene of the crime.

It is not difficult by taking one piece of circumstantial evidence out of context to demolish the veracity of that single bit of evidence. Taking an overview of all the cumulative available evidence however, we pass from a hypothesis, to a possibility, then to a probability and ultimately to a certainty.

You see, if you are determined to disbelieve then there is hardly anything which is really proveable. Stretch the long arm of coincidence far enough and you can disprove almost anything.

In our imaginary court case there would come a time when circumstantial evidence would become so overwhelming that no REASONABLE and unbiased person would NOT bring a verdict of guilty. We all realise that coincidence cannot go on forever — except when we wish to disbelieve something!

The evidence for the Virgin Mary having lived and died in Britain seems to be as unassailable as we can expect such evidence to be.